D1824493

THE DAILY
READING BIBLE

Volume 13

LUKE 1-6   AMOS   2 CORINTHIANS

The Daily Reading Bible (Volume 13)
© Matthias Media 2008

Matthias Media
(St Matthias Press Ltd ACN 067 558 365)
PO Box 225
Kingsford NSW 2032
Australia
Ph: (02) 9663 1478; Int. +61-2-9663-1478
Fax: (02) 9663 3265; Int. +61-2-9663-3265
Email: info@matthiasmedia.com.au
Internet: www.matthiasmedia.com.au

Matthias Media (USA)
Ph: 724 964 8152; Int. +1-724-964-8152
Fax: 724 964 8166; Int. +1-724-964-8166
Email: sales@matthiasmedia.com
Internet: www.matthiasmedia.com

All Scripture is taken from the Holy Bible, English Standard Version, copyright © 2001 by Crossway Bibles, a publishing ministry of Good News Publishers. Used by permission. All rights reserved.

ISBN 978 1 921441 01 1

All rights reserved. Except as may be permitted by the Copyright Act, no part of this publication may be reproduced in any form or by any means without prior permission from the publisher.

Cover design and typesetting by Matthias Media.

CONTENTS

INTRODUCTION

Reading our Bibles regularly is getting harder. That, at least, seems to be the common experience of many Christians. We could waste lots of ink speculating on the reasons for this: is it the frenetic pace of life these days? Is it spiritual laziness? Is it the impact of postmodernism on our culture and the lack of certainty when it comes to interpreting the written word?

But a better option than speculating on the reasons, we thought, was to provide a new resource for Christians to help them get back into a more regular habit of reflecting daily on God's word. So back in June 2001, we decided to start including a section called 'Bible Brief' in our monthly magazine, *The Briefing* (see www.matthiasmedia.com.au for more information about *The Briefing*). The 'Bible Brief' provided 20 short readings each month—acknowledging that there will be days we miss or days when we want to do something a bit different—with questions, thoughts to ponder, and suggestions to get started in prayer.

Now, several years later, we have a good collection of 'Bible Briefs', and it's time to offer them to a wider audience in a format that will, we hope, be even more convenient and useful.

This thirteenth volume contains 60 readings, all designed to be done in 15–20 minutes. These daily Bible readings are designed to help you feed regularly from God's word. They won't cover every issue in each passage, nor even every passage from each Bible book. In other words, *they are no substitute for the in-depth study of the Scriptures* that you may undertake personally, in small groups or through listening to sermons.

With the kind permission of our friends at Crossway Bibles, we've been able to make this a complete package to take with you—we've included the English Standard Version Bible text with each daily study. So you can take this one book with you and have everything you need—on the train, on the bus, or to the park at lunchtime—wherever and whenever you can get 20 minutes to yourself.

How to use these readings
- *With a penitent heart*, the true prerequisite for all Bible reading. Open with prayer (perhaps using the prayer suggested at the beginning of each set of studies).
- *With 15–20 minutes* of peace and quiet. If you can take longer, and want to read and pray further—great! But we have designed the readings to be done in a fairly short space of time.
- *With an accurate modern translation.* We recommend and have included the new ESV translation. The writers of the studies refer to this translation. Contact us for further details about the ESV or visit www.matthiasmedia.com.au/ESV

- *With a pen*. Even if you only jot down brief ideas, writing focuses the mind.
- *As a guide and help, not a straitjacket.* Feel free to dig further into the passage, to notice and ponder things that the questions don't point to.
- *As a launch-pad for prayer.* Use the prayer ideas at the end of each reading as a starting point for your daily prayer. Many of the points that will arise from the readings will be things you can pray for yourself, and also for others (family, friends, neighbours, etc.). Why not compile a list of people you want to pray for (you can write them in the blank space below), and use the prayer ideas from each reading to pray for the next person on your list?

This thirteenth volume includes:
- studies on Luke 1-6 (written by Andrew Richardson, senior minister at Scots Presbyterian Church, Brisbane)
- studies on Amos (written by Simon Flinders, assistant minister at St Thomas' Anglican Church, North Sydney)
- studies on 2 Corinthians (written by James Warren, senior pastor of the 7fifteen congregation and Ministry Training Strategy coordinator at St Paul's Carlingford).

Matthias Media
March 2008

Please note: the main section of Scripture for each study is reproduced before the questions. Other Scripture references are reproduced as footnotes at the bottom of the page, or, where the passages are too long to be included as footnotes, in the Appendix.

PEOPLE TO PRAY FOR:

LUKE 1-6

INTRODUCTION

There are always rumours and legends that spring up around any famous person. The supposed sightings of Elvis Presley after his death are a classic example. Luke's aim in writing his Gospel is to cut through any rumours and legends about the life of Jesus Christ, and to give his friend Theophilus certainty about who Jesus really is. God-willing, as you read through the first six chapters of Luke, you too will become more certain about Jesus Christ, and grow more confident in your faith in him.

You might like to use this prayer (or your own variation on it) before each of the next 20 studies:

God my Saviour,
Help me to read Luke humbly. Help me to be hungry to be fed by your word. Please make me more certain about your son Jesus Christ so that I may serve him and trust him as my lord and king.
Amen.

NB: Tick the box when you've completed each study ✓

READING 1   LUKE 1:1-4

Inasmuch as many have undertaken to compile a narrative of the things that have been accomplished among us, [2] just as those who from the beginning were eyewitnesses and ministers of the word have delivered them to us, [3] it seemed good to me also, having followed all things closely for some time past, to write an orderly account for you, most excellent Theophilus, [4] that you may have certainty concerning the things you have been taught.

1. What kind of account does Luke want to write about the things he's heard?

orderly

2. Where is Luke's information coming from?

his own observations and experiences

3. What is Luke's aim in writing? *That Theophilus may be certain of who Jesus is.*

PONDER How certain are you about who Jesus is? What kind of confidence does Luke inspire as a historian and biographer? *— He was a follower, a doctor*

PRAYER IDEAS Thank God for Luke's careful work in recording Jesus' life. Ask him to make you more certain about Jesus' work and identity as you read through Luke 1-6.

In the days of Herod, king of Judea, there was a priest named Zechariah, of the division of Abijah. And he had a wife from the daughters of Aaron, and her name was Elizabeth. 6 And they were both righteous before God, walking blamelessly in all the commandments and statutes of the Lord. 7 But they had no child, because Elizabeth was barren, and both were advanced in years.

8 Now while he was serving as priest before God when his division was on duty, 9 according to the custom of the priesthood, he was chosen by lot to enter the temple of the Lord and burn incense. 10 And the whole multitude of the people were praying outside at the hour of incense. 11 And there appeared to him an angel of the Lord standing on the right side of the altar of incense. 12 And Zechariah was troubled when he saw him, and fear fell upon him. 13 But the angel said to him, "Do not be afraid, Zechariah, for your prayer has been heard, and your wife Elizabeth will bear you a son, and you shall call his name John. 14 And you will have joy and gladness, and many will rejoice at his birth, 15 for he will be great before the Lord. And he must not drink wine or strong drink, and he will be filled with the Holy Spirit, even from his mother's womb. 16 And he will turn many of the children of Israel to the Lord their God, 17 and he will go before him in the spirit and power of Elijah, to turn the hearts of the fathers to the children, and the disobedient to the wisdom of the just, to make ready for the Lord a people prepared." 18 And Zechariah said to the angel, "How

shall I know this? For I am an old man, and my wife is advanced in years." 19 And the angel answered him, "I am Gabriel. I stand in the presence of God, and I was sent to speak to you and to bring you this good news. 20 And behold, you will be silent and unable to speak until the day that these things take place, because you did not believe my words, which will be fulfilled in their time." 21 And the people were waiting for Zechariah, and they were wondering at his delay in the temple. 22 And when he came out, he was unable to speak to them, and they realized that he had seen a vision in the temple. And he kept making signs to them and remained mute. 23 And when his time of service was ended, he went to his home.

24 After these days his wife Elizabeth conceived, and for five months she kept herself hidden, saying, 25 "Thus the Lord has done for me in the days when he looked on me, to take away my reproach among people."

1. Which Old Testament events and people are brought to mind by Zechariah's and Elizabeth's experiences? (Hint: See Genesis 17:15-21,¹ and Judges 13:2-24 in the Appendix, pp. 67-68.)

---

1. And God said to Abraham, "As for Sarai your wife, you shall not call her name Sarai, but Sarah shall be her name. 16 I will bless her, and moreover, I will give you a son by her. I will bless her, and she shall become nations; kings of peoples shall come from her." 17 Then Abraham fell on his face and laughed and said to himself, "Shall a child be born to a man who is a hundred years old? Shall Sarah, who is ninety years old, bear a child?" 18 And Abraham said to God, "Oh that Ishmael might live before you!" 19 God said, "No, but Sarah your wife shall bear you a son, and you shall call his name Isaac. I will establish my covenant with him as an everlasting covenant for his offspring after him. 20 As for Ishmael, I have heard you; behold, I have blessed him and will make him fruitful and multiply him greatly. He shall father twelve princes, and I will make him into a great nation. 21 But I will establish my covenant with Isaac, whom Sarah shall bear to you at this time next year."

2. In the light of these Old Testament experiences, why should Zechariah have known better than to doubt the angel's promise?

3. How does this account emphasize God's faithfulness to his promises?

PONDER How does this account give you greater confidence in God's faithfulness to his plans? What expectations about Jesus does this passage raise?

PRAYER IDEAS Ask God to help you trust in his promises, even when they seem outlandish.

READING 3   LUKE 1:26-38

In the sixth month the angel Gabriel was sent from God to a city of Galilee named Nazareth, 27 to a virgin betrothed to a man whose name was Joseph, of the house of David. And the virgin's name was Mary. 28 And he came to her and said, "Greetings, O favored one, the Lord is with you!" 29 But she was greatly troubled at the saying, and tried to discern what sort of greeting this might be. 30 And the angel said to her, "Do not be afraid, Mary, for you have found favor with God. 31 And behold, you will conceive in your womb and bear a son, and you shall call his name Jesus. 32 He will be great and will be called the Son of the Most High. And the Lord God will give to him the throne of his father David, 33 and he will reign over the house of Jacob forever, and of his kingdom there will be no end."

34 And Mary said to the angel, "How will this be, since I am a virgin?"

35 And the angel answered her, "The Holy Spirit will come upon you, and the power of the Most High will overshadow you; therefore the child to be born will be called holy—the Son of God. 36 And behold, your relative Elizabeth in her old age has also conceived a son, and this is the sixth month with her who was called barren. 37 For nothing will be impossible with God." 38 And

Mary said, "Behold, I am the servant of the Lord; let it be to me according to your word." And the angel departed from her.

1. How is the announcement to Mary connected to the announcement to Zechariah? What expectations does this connection raise?

2. What are the key things the angel announces about Jesus?

3. How does Mary respond to the angel's announcement?

PONDER Do you think Mary's response to the angel was appropriate? Is her response the same as your response to God's word?

PRAYER IDEAS Thank God for sending Jesus, the great "Son of the Most High" (v. 32), to reign over his kingdom forever. Ask God to make you as willing as Mary to be part of his plans.

READING 4   LUKE 1:39-56 ■

In those days Mary arose and went with haste into the hill country, to a town in Judah, 40 and she entered the house of Zechariah and greeted Elizabeth. 41 And when Elizabeth heard the greeting of Mary, the baby leaped in her womb. And Elizabeth was filled with the Holy Spirit, 42 and she exclaimed with a loud cry, "Blessed are you among women, and blessed is the fruit of your womb! 43 And why is this granted to me that the mother of my Lord should come to me? 44 For behold, when the sound of your greeting came to my ears, the baby in my womb leaped for joy. 45 And blessed is she who believed that there would be a fulfillment of what was spoken to her from the Lord."

46 And Mary said,

"My soul magnifies the Lord,
    47 and my spirit rejoices in God my
        Savior,
48 for he has looked on the humble estate
        of his servant.
    For behold, from now on all generations
        will call me blessed;
49 for he who is mighty has done great
        things for me,
    and holy is his name.
50 And his mercy is for those who fear him
        from generation to generation.
51 He has shown strength with his arm;
    he has scattered the proud in the
        thoughts of their hearts;
52 he has brought down the mighty from
        their thrones
    and exalted those of humble estate;

53 he has filled the hungry with good things,
    and the rich he has sent away empty.
54 He has helped his servant Israel,
    in remembrance of his mercy,
55 as he spoke to our fathers,
    to Abraham and to his offspring
        forever."

56 And Mary remained with her about three months and returned to her home.

1. What does this passage tell you about Mary's and Elizabeth's respective sons?

2. According to Mary's song, how has God treated her?

3. What does the second half of Mary's song tell you about God's treatment of people generally?

PONDER Mary celebrates the fact that God brings down the proud and self-sufficient, and exalts the humble and needy. How do you think Jesus will do these things in the rest of Luke's Gospel?

PRAYER IDEAS Make Mary's song your prayer today as you thank God for his mercy to the humble and needy.

Now the time came for Elizabeth to give birth, and she bore a son. [58] And her neighbors and relatives heard that the Lord had shown great mercy to her, and they rejoiced with her. [59] And on the eighth day they came to circumcise the child. And they would have called him Zechariah after his father, [60] but his mother answered, "No; he shall be called John." [61] And they said to her, "None of your relatives is called by this name." [62] And they made signs to his father, inquiring what he wanted him to be called. [63] And he asked for a writing tablet and wrote, "His name is John." And they all wondered. [64] And immediately his mouth was opened and his tongue loosed, and he spoke, blessing God. [65] And fear came on all their neighbors. And all these things were talked about through all the hill country of Judea, [66] and all who heard them laid them up in their hearts, saying, "What then will this child be?" For the hand of the Lord was with him.

[67] And his father Zechariah was filled with the Holy Spirit and prophesied, saying,

[68] "Blessed be the Lord God of Israel,
    for he has visited and redeemed his
        people
[69] and has raised up a horn of salvation for us
    in the house of his servant David,
[70] as he spoke by the mouth of his holy
        prophets from of old,
[71] that we should be saved from our enemies
    and from the hand of all who hate us;
[72] to show the mercy promised to our
        fathers
    and to remember his holy covenant,
[73] the oath that he swore to our father
        Abraham, to grant us
[74] that we, being delivered from the
        hand of our enemies,
might serve him without fear,
[75] in holiness and righteousness before
        him all our days.

[76] And you, child, will be called the prophet
        of the Most High;
    for you will go before the Lord to
        prepare his ways,
[77] to give knowledge of salvation to his
        people
    in the forgiveness of their sins,
[78] because of the tender mercy of our God,
    whereby the sunrise shall visit us from
        on high
[79] to give light to those who sit in darkness
    and in the shadow of death,
    to guide our feet into the way of peace."

[80] And the child grew and became strong in spirit, and he was in the wilderness until the day of his public appearance to Israel.

1. How does John's birth confirm God's faithfulness to his word?

2. After Zechariah is able to speak again, who are his first words about? What does this tell you about Zechariah's priorities?

3. According to verses 74-75 and 78-79, what is God going to do for his people?

PONDER How does Jesus fulfil the promises expressed in verses 74-75 and 78-79? Is this your experience of the Christian life?

PRAYER IDEAS Thank God for the wonderful freedom you have through Jesus to serve God "without fear, in holiness and righteousness before him all [your] days" (vv. 74-75).

In those days a decree went out from Caesar Augustus that all the world should be registered. [2] This was the first registration when Quirinius was governor of Syria. [3] And all went to be registered, each to his own town. [4] And Joseph also went up from Galilee, from the town of Nazareth, to Judea, to the city of David, which is called Bethlehem, because he was of the house and lineage of David, [5] to be registered with Mary, his betrothed, who was with child. [6] And while they were there, the time came for her to give birth. [7] And she gave birth to her firstborn son and wrapped him in swaddling cloths and laid him in a manger, because there was no place for them in the inn.

1. What is the extent of Caesar Augustus's power?

2. What is the state of the royal house of David at this time? How does it compare to the things that have been prophesied

about it in 1:32-33[2] and 1:68-71?[3]

3. What are the conditions surrounding the birth of Mary's son? Given what we have already learnt about Jesus and God's Messiah in the preceding chapters, are they appropriate?

PONDER Looking at Jesus Christ and Caesar Augustus from a worldly perspective, what is the extent of Jesus' power and glory compared to Augustus' in this passage? How does this change when you look at them from God's perspective?

PRAYER IDEAS Ask God to help you accept the Lord Jesus on his terms, however unexpected they might be.

And in the same region there were shepherds out in the field, keeping watch over their flock by night. [9] And an angel of the Lord appeared to them, and the glory of the Lord shone around them, and they were filled with fear. [10] And the angel said to them, "Fear not, for behold, I bring you good news of great joy that will be for all the people. [11] For unto you is born this day in the city of David a Savior, who

is Christ the Lord. [12] And this will be a sign for you: you will find a baby wrapped in swaddling cloths and lying in a manger." [13] And suddenly there was with the angel a multitude of the heavenly host praising God and saying,

[14] "Glory to God in the highest,
   and on earth peace among those with
      whom he is pleased!"

---

2. "He will be great and will be called the Son of the Most High. And the Lord God will give to him the throne of his father David, [33] and he will reign over the house of Jacob forever, and of his kingdom there will be no end."
3. "Blessed be the Lord God of Israel,
   for he has visited and redeemed his people

[69] and has raised up a horn of salvation for us
   in the house of his servant David,
[70] as he spoke by the mouth of his holy prophets from of
      old,
[71] that we should be saved from our enemies
   and from the hand of all who hate us ..."

15 When the angels went away from them into heaven, the shepherds said to one another, "Let us go over to Bethlehem and see this thing that has happened, which the Lord has made known to us." 16 And they went with haste and found Mary and Joseph, and the baby lying in a manger. 17 And when they saw it, they made known the saying that had been told them concerning this child. 18 And all who heard it wondered at what the shepherds told them. 19 But Mary treasured up all these things, pondering them in her heart. 20 And the shepherds returned, glorifying and praising God for all they had heard and seen, as it had been told them.

21 And at the end of eight days, when he was circumcised, he was called Jesus, the name given by the angel before he was conceived in the womb.

1. *What does the presence of the angels tell you about the nature of the event of Jesus' birth?*

2. *What does the angel say about Jesus in verse 11?*

3. *How do the shepherds respond?*

PONDER How does this passage provide more certainty that Jesus is God's king, the Christ? Following on from the previous reading, what hints are there in this passage that he is no ordinary king?

PRAYER IDEAS Give thanks with joy for the good news of Jesus' birth.

READING 8   LUKE 2:22-40 ▮

And when the time came for their purification according to the Law of Moses, they brought him up to Jerusalem to present him to the Lord 23 (as it is written in the Law of the Lord, "Every male who first opens the womb shall be called holy to the Lord") 24 and to offer a sacrifice according to what is said in the Law of the Lord, "a pair of turtledoves, or two young pigeons." 25 Now there was a man in Jerusalem, whose name was Simeon, and this man was righteous and devout, waiting for the consolation of Israel, and the Holy Spirit was upon him. 26 And it had been revealed to him by the Holy Spirit that he would not see death before he had seen the Lord's Christ. 27 And he came in the Spirit into the temple, and when the parents brought in the child Jesus, to do for him according to the custom of the Law, 28 he took him up in his arms and blessed God and said,

29 "Lord, now you are letting your servant
depart in peace,
according to your word;
30 for my eyes have seen your salvation
31 that you have prepared in the
presence of all peoples,
32 a light for revelation to the Gentiles,
and for glory to your people Israel."

33 And his father and his mother marveled at what was said about him. 34 And Simeon blessed them and said to Mary his mother, "Behold, this child is appointed for the fall and rising of many in Israel, and for a sign that is opposed 35 (and a sword will pierce through your own soul also), so that

thoughts from many hearts may be revealed." 36 And there was a prophetess, Anna, the daughter of Phanuel, of the tribe of Asher. She was advanced in years, having lived with her husband seven years from when she was a virgin, 37 and then as a widow until she was eighty-four. She did not depart from the temple, worshiping with fasting and prayer night and day. 38 And coming up at that very hour she began to give thanks to God and to speak of him to all who were waiting for the redemption of Jerusalem.

39 And when they had performed everything according to the Law of the Lord, they returned into Galilee, to their own town of Nazareth. 40 And the child grew and became strong, filled with wisdom. And the favor of God was upon him.

1. What does Simeon say about Jesus?

2. How does Anna respond to Jesus?

3. How do their claims about Jesus increase your confidence that he is God's saviour and redeemer?

PONDER Simeon and Anna are thrilled to see God's plans for the salvation of the world coming to fruition. Do you share their excitement?

PRAYER IDEAS Thank God for fulfilling his plans for the salvation of the world in Jesus. Ask him to help you share Simeon and Anna's excitement at what he has done.

READING 9 — LUKE 2:41-52

Now his parents went to Jerusalem every year at the Feast of the Passover. 42 And when he was twelve years old, they went up according to custom. 43 And when the feast was ended, as they were returning, the boy Jesus stayed behind in Jerusalem. His parents did not know it, 44 but supposing him to be in the group they went a day's journey, but then they began to search for him among their relatives and acquaintances, 45 and when they did not find him, they returned to Jerusalem, searching for him. 46 After three days they found him in the temple, sitting among the teachers, listening to them and asking them questions. 47 And all who heard him were amazed at his understanding and his answers. 48 And when his parents saw him, they were astonished. And his mother said to him, "Son, why have you treated us so? Behold, your father and I have been searching for you in great distress." 49 And he said to them, "Why were you looking for me? Did you not know that I must be in my Father's house?" 50 And they did not understand the saying that he spoke to them. 51 And he went down with them and came to Nazareth and was submissive to them. And his mother treasured up all these things in her heart.

52 And Jesus increased in wisdom and in stature and in favor with God and man.

1. What is Jesus doing when his parents find him in Jerusalem?

2. What does Jesus' reply in verse 49 tell you about his understanding of who he was?

3. How does Luke summarize Jesus' childhood?

PONDER What particular aspect of Jesus' identity does this account highlight? Are you ready to listen to Jesus' teaching with the same amazement as the people in the temple?

PRAYER IDEAS Ask God to help you listen to and accept Jesus' teaching, especially as you continue reading Luke.

READING 10   LUKE 3:1-22

In the fifteenth year of the reign of Tiberius Caesar, Pontius Pilate being governor of Judea, and Herod being tetrarch of Galilee, and his brother Philip tetrarch of the region of Ituraea and Trachonitis, and Lysanias tetrarch of Abilene, 2 during the high priesthood of Annas and Caiaphas, the word of God came to John the son of Zechariah in the wilderness. 3 And he went into all the region around the Jordan, proclaiming a baptism of repentance for the forgiveness of sins. 4 As it is written in the book of the words of Isaiah the prophet,

"The voice of one crying in the wilderness:
'Prepare the way of the Lord,
   make his paths straight.
5 Every valley shall be filled,
   and every mountain and hill shall be
      made low,
and the crooked shall become straight,
   and the rough places shall become level
      ways,
6 and all flesh shall see the salvation of
      God.'"

7 He said therefore to the crowds that came out to be baptized by him, "You brood of vipers! Who warned you to flee from the wrath to come? 8 Bear fruits in keeping with repentance. And do not begin to say to yourselves, 'We have Abraham as our father.' For I tell you, God is able from these stones to raise up children for Abraham. 9 Even now the axe is laid to the root of the trees. Every tree therefore that does not bear good fruit is cut down and thrown into the fire."

10 And the crowds asked him, "What then shall we do?" 11 And he answered them, "Whoever has two tunics is to share with him who has none, and whoever has food is to do likewise." 12 Tax collectors also came to be baptized and said to him, "Teacher, what shall we do?" 13 And he said to them, "Collect no more than you are authorized to do." 14 Soldiers also asked him, "And we, what shall we do?" And he said to them, "Do not extort money from anyone by threats or by false accusation, and be content with your wages."

15 As the people were in expectation, and all were questioning in their hearts

concerning John, whether he might be the Christ, ¹⁶ John answered them all, saying, "I baptize you with water, but he who is mightier than I is coming, the strap of whose sandals I am not worthy to untie. He will baptize you with the Holy Spirit and with fire. ¹⁷ His winnowing fork is in his hand, to clear his threshing floor and to gather the wheat into his barn, but the chaff he will burn with unquenchable fire."

¹⁸ So with many other exhortations he preached good news to the people. ¹⁹ But Herod the tetrarch, who had been reproved by him for Herodias, his brother's wife, and for all the evil things that Herod had done, ²⁰ added this to them all, that he locked up John in prison.

²¹ Now when all the people were baptized, and when Jesus also had been baptized and was praying, the heavens were opened, ²² and the Holy Spirit descended on him in bodily form, like a dove; and a voice came from heaven, "You are my beloved Son; with you I am well pleased."

1. What is John's role in God's plans (cf. 1:14-17)?[4]

2. According to John's instructions, how are people to prepare for the coming of the Christ?

3. What does John's teaching and Jesus' baptism tell you about Jesus?

PONDER John is very much an Old Testament-style prophet. His teaching highlights that Jesus is not only a saviour, he is also a judge who will punish those who have rejected God's ways. What makes John's message an uncomfortable one for people then and now?

PRAYER IDEAS Ask God to help you take John's teaching about Jesus seriously.

READING 11   LUKE 3:23-38

Jesus, when he began his ministry, was about thirty years of age, being the son (as was supposed) of Joseph, the son of Heli, ²⁴ the son of Matthat, the son of Levi, the son of Melchi, the son of Jannai, the son of Joseph, ²⁵ the son of Mattathias, the son of Amos, the son of Nahum, the son of Esli, the son of Naggai, ²⁶ the son of Maath, the son of Mattathias, the son of Semein, the son of Josech, the son of Joda, ²⁷ the son of Joanan, the son of Rhesa, the son of Zerubbabel, the son of Shealtiel,

---

4. "And you will have joy and gladness, and many will rejoice at his birth, ¹⁵ for he will be great before the Lord. And he must not drink wine or strong drink, and he will be filled with the Holy Spirit, even from his mother's womb. ¹⁶ And he will turn many of the children of Israel to the Lord their God, ¹⁷ and he will go before him in the spirit and power of Elijah, to turn the hearts of the fathers to the children, and the disobedient to the wisdom of the just, to make ready for the Lord a people prepared."

the son of Neri, [28] the son of Melchi, the son of Addi, the son of Cosam, the son of Elmadam, the son of Er, [29] the son of Joshua, the son of Eliezer, the son of Jorim, the son of Matthat, the son of Levi, [30] the son of Simeon, the son of Judah, the son of Joseph, the son of Jonam, the son of Eliakim, [31] the son of Melea, the son of Menna, the son of Mattatha, the son of Nathan, the son of David, [32] the son of Jesse, the son of Obed, the son of Boaz, the son of Sala, the son of Nahshon, [33] the son of Amminadab, the son of Admin, the son of Arni, the son of Hezron, the son of Perez, the son of Judah, [34] the son of Jacob, the son of Isaac, the son of Abraham, the son of Terah, the son of Nahor, [35] the son of Serug, the son of Reu, the son of Peleg, the son of Eber, the son of Shelah, [36] the son of Cainan, the son of Arphaxad, the son of Shem, the son of Noah, the son of Lamech, [37] the son of Methuselah, the son of Enoch, the son of Jared, the son of Mahalaleel, the son of Cainan, [38] the son of Enos, the son of Seth, the son of Adam, the son of God.

1. What does the genealogy highlight about Jesus' relationship to Joseph?

2. Out of all the names, which five are the most important and why?

3. What claims about Jesus does the genealogy support (cf. Luke 1:32-33,[5] 69,[6] 73[7])?

PONDER For a Jewish genealogy of Luke's time, starting with God is very unusual. It highlights a comparison between the first 'son of God' (i.e. Adam) and the new 'son of God' (Jesus). How is Jesus a better son of God than Adam?

PRAYER IDEAS Give thanks that God has sent another son to rescue humanity from the disastrous situation created by his first son, Adam, and Adam's descendants.

READING 12 — LUKE 4:1-13

And Jesus, full of the Holy Spirit, returned from the Jordan and was led by the Spirit in the wilderness [2] for forty days, being tempted by the devil. And he ate nothing during those days. And when they were ended, he was hungry. [3] The devil said to him, "If you are the Son of God, command this stone to become bread." [4] And Jesus answered him, "It is written, 'Man shall not live by bread alone.'" [5] And the devil took him up and showed him all the kingdoms of the world in a moment of time, [6] and said to him, "To you I will give all this authority and their glory, for it has been delivered to me, and I give it to whom I will. [7] If you, then, will worship me, it will all be yours." [8] And Jesus answered him, "It is written,

---

5. "He will be great and will be called the Son of the Most High. And the Lord God will give to him the throne of his father David, [33] and he will reign over the house of Jacob forever, and of his kingdom there will be no end."

6. "... and has raised up a horn of salvation for us
    in the house of his servant David ..."

7. "... the oath that he swore to our father Abraham, to grant us ..."

"'You shall worship the Lord your God,
and him only shall you serve.'"

9 And he took him to Jerusalem and set him on the pinnacle of the temple and said to him, "If you are the Son of God, throw yourself down from here, 10 for it is written,

"'He will command his angels concerning you,
to guard you,'

11 and

"'On their hands they will bear you up,
lest you strike your foot against a stone.'"

12 And Jesus answered him, "It is said, 'You shall not put the Lord your God to the test.'" 13 And when the devil had ended every temptation, he departed from him until an opportune time.

1. *Which part of Israel's history is brought to mind by this passage? (Hint: see Deut 8:1-3,[8] 6:12-16.[9])*

2. *How is Jesus' reaction to temptation different from Israel's (cf. Num 14:2-5[10] and Exod 32:1-4[11])?*

3. *If Jesus had given in to the devil's third temptation (vv. 9-11), how would it have affected his mission?*

PONDER

What particular temptations are you dealing with at the moment? Read Hebrews 4:15-16.[12] How is the account of Jesus' temptation comforting and encouraging?

PRAYER IDEAS

Give thanks that Jesus understood temptation but never gave in. Ask for his help in your own struggle with sin.

---

8. "The whole commandment that I command you today you shall be careful to do, that you may live and multiply, and go in and possess the land that the Lord swore to give to your fathers. 2 And you shall remember the whole way that the Lord your God has led you these forty years in the wilderness, that he might humble you, testing you to know what was in your heart, whether you would keep his commandments or not. 3 And he humbled you and let you hunger and fed you with manna, which you did not know, nor did your fathers know, that he might make you know that man does not live by bread alone, but man lives by every word that comes from the mouth of the Lord."

9. "... then take care lest you forget the Lord, who brought you out of the land of Egypt, out of the house of slavery. 13 It is the Lord your God you shall fear. Him you shall serve and by his name you shall swear. 14 You shall not go after other gods, the gods of the peoples who are around you— 15 for the Lord your God in your midst is a jealous God—lest the anger of the Lord your God be kindled against you, and he destroy you from off the face of the earth.

16 "You shall not put the Lord your God to the test, as you tested him at Massah."

10. And all the people of Israel grumbled against Moses and Aaron. The whole congregation said to them, "Would that we had died in the land of Egypt! Or would that we had died in

this wilderness! 3 Why is the Lord bringing us into this land, to fall by the sword? Our wives and our little ones will become a prey. Would it not be better for us to go back to Egypt?" 4 And they said to one another, "Let us choose a leader and go back to Egypt."

5 Then Moses and Aaron fell on their faces before all the assembly of the congregation of the people of Israel.

11. When the people saw that Moses delayed to come down from the mountain, the people gathered themselves together to Aaron and said to him, "Up, make us gods who shall go before us. As for this Moses, the man who brought us up out of the land of Egypt, we do not know what has become of him." 2 So Aaron said to them, "Take off the rings of gold that are in the ears of your wives, your sons, and your daughters, and bring them to me." 3 So all the people took off the rings of gold that were in their ears and brought them to Aaron. 4 And he received the gold from their hand and fashioned it with a graving tool and made a golden calf. And they said, "These are your gods, O Israel, who brought you up out of the land of Egypt!"

12. For we do not have a high priest who is unable to sympathize with our weaknesses, but one who in every respect has been tempted as we are, yet without sin. 16 Let us then with confidence draw near to the throne of grace, that we may receive mercy and find grace to help in time of need.

And Jesus returned in the power of the Spirit to Galilee, and a report about him went out through all the surrounding country. 15 And he taught in their synagogues, being glorified by all.

16 And he came to Nazareth, where he had been brought up. And as was his custom, he went to the synagogue on the Sabbath day, and he stood up to read. 17 And the scroll of the prophet Isaiah was given to him. He unrolled the scroll and found the place where it was written,

18 "The Spirit of the Lord is upon me,
    because he has anointed me
        to proclaim good news to the poor.
He has sent me to proclaim liberty to the
            captives
    and recovering of sight to the blind,
        to set at liberty those who are
            oppressed,
19 to proclaim the year of the Lord's favor."

20 And he rolled up the scroll and gave it back to the attendant and sat down. And the eyes of all in the synagogue were fixed on him. 21 And he began to say to them, "Today this Scripture has been fulfilled in your hearing." 22 And all spoke well of him and marveled at the gracious words that were coming from his mouth. And they said, "Is not this Joseph's son?" 23 And he said to them, "Doubtless you will quote to me this proverb, 'Physician, heal yourself.' What we have heard you did at Capernaum, do here in your hometown as well." 24 And he said, "Truly, I say to you, no prophet is acceptable in his hometown. 25 But in truth, I tell you, there were many widows in Israel in the days of Elijah, when the heavens were shut up three years and six months, and a great famine came over all the land, 26 and Elijah was sent to none of them but only to Zarephath, in the land of Sidon, to a woman who was a widow. 27 And there were many lepers in Israel in the time of the prophet Elisha, and none of them was cleansed, but only Naaman the Syrian." 28 When they heard these things, all in the synagogue were filled with wrath. 29 And they rose up and drove him out of the town and brought him to the brow of the hill on which their town was built, so that they could throw him down the cliff. 30 But passing through their midst, he went away.

1. According to the quote Jesus reads from Isaiah (vv. 18-19), who is going to benefit from the Messiah's mission?

2. What important claim does Jesus make in verse 21?

3. The people's remark "Is not this Joseph's son?" is not a putdown but a statement of ownership. What they mean is, "You're a Nazareth boy with special obligations to us". How does Jesus respond? Why does his response make them want to kill him? (Hint: see pointer on p. 20.)

PONDER What does Jesus mean by "the poor", "the captives", "the blind" and "the oppressed"? (Check out the original context of Jesus' quote in Isaiah 61 in the Appendix, p. 68.) Do you ever make the mistake of thinking that Jesus is obligated to you because of your background, your life or your standing in the Christian community?

PRAYER IDEAS Give thanks that Jesus brought the year of God's favour, and ask God to help you to keep on remembering that you enjoy God's favour through his generosity, not his obligation.

POINTER Sidon (v. 26) and Syria (v. 27) were not part of Israel.

READING 14   LUKE 4:31-44

And he went down to Capernaum, a city of Galilee. And he was teaching them on the Sabbath, 32 and they were astonished at his teaching, for his word possessed authority. 33 And in the synagogue there was a man who had the spirit of an unclean demon, and he cried out with a loud voice, 34 "Ha! What have you to do with us, Jesus of Nazareth? Have you come to destroy us? I know who you are—the Holy One of God." 35 But Jesus rebuked him, saying, "Be silent and come out of him!" And when the demon had thrown him down in their midst, he came out of him, having done him no harm. 36 And they were all amazed and said to one another, "What is this word? For with authority and power he commands the unclean spirits, and they come out!" 37 And reports about him went out into every place in the surrounding region.

38 And he arose and left the synagogue and entered Simon's house. Now Simon's mother-in-law was ill with a high fever, and they appealed to him on her behalf. 39 And he stood over her and rebuked the fever, and it left her, and immediately she rose and began to serve them.

40 Now when the sun was setting, all those who had any who were sick with various diseases brought them to him, and he laid his hands on every one of them and healed them. 41 And demons also came out of many, crying, "You are the Son of God!" But he rebuked them and would not allow them to speak, because they knew that he was the Christ.

42 And when it was day, he departed and went into a desolate place. And the people sought him and came to him, and would have kept him from leaving them, 43 but he said to them, "I must preach the good news of the kingdom of God to the other towns as well; for I was sent for this purpose." 44 And he was preaching in the synagogues of Judea.

1. How do Jesus' actions in these verses fulfil his mission of proclaiming good news to the poor, the captives, the blind and the oppressed?

2. What is Jesus' top priority (v. 43)?

3. What kind of authority and power does Jesus display in these verses?

PONDER Jesus' mission to the poor, the captives, the blind and the oppressed (see Reading 13) could be interpreted to mean that his primary interest is in giving people a better life in this world. What does this passage tell you about Jesus' actions and priorities? What do you think is his primary interest?

PRAYER IDEAS Give thanks for Jesus' authority over sickness and evil spirits. Ask God to help you make Jesus' priorities your priorities.

READING 15   LUKE 5:1-11

On one occasion, while the crowd was pressing in on him to hear the word of God, he was standing by the lake of Gennesaret, 2 and he saw two boats by the lake, but the fishermen had gone out of them and were washing their nets. 3 Getting into one of the boats, which was Simon's, he asked him to put out a little from the land. And he sat down and taught the people from the boat. 4 And when he had finished speaking, he said to Simon, "Put out into the deep and let down your nets for a catch." 5 And Simon answered, "Master, we toiled all night and took nothing! But at your word I will let down the nets." 6 And when they had done this, they enclosed a large number of fish, and their nets were breaking. 7 They signaled to their partners in the other boat to come and help them. And they came and filled both the boats, so that they began to sink. 8 But when Simon Peter saw it, he fell down at Jesus' knees, saying, "Depart from me, for I am a sinful man, O Lord." 9 For he and all who were with him were astonished at the catch of fish that they had taken, 10 and so also were James and John, sons of Zebedee, who were partners with Simon. And Jesus said to Simon, "Do not be afraid; from now on you will be catching men." 11 And when they had brought their boats to land, they left everything and followed him.

1. How does Simon's relationship with Jesus change over the course of this passage?

2. What mission does Jesus have for Peter?

3. How do Peter, James and John express their acceptance of Jesus' authority?

PONDER How would you characterize your relationship with Jesus? How does it compare with the fishermen in this passage?

PRAYER IDEAS Ask God to help you to be prepared to leave anything (or everything) to follow the Lord Jesus.

While he was in one of the cities, there came a man full of leprosy. And when he saw Jesus, he fell on his face and begged him, "Lord, if you will, you can make me clean." 13 And Jesus stretched out his hand and touched him, saying, "I will; be clean." And immediately the leprosy left him. 14 And he charged him to tell no one, but "go and show yourself to the priest, and make an offering for your cleansing, as Moses commanded, for a proof to them." 15 But now even more the report about him went abroad, and great crowds gathered to hear him and to be healed of their infirmities. 16 But he would withdraw to desolate places and pray.

17 On one of those days, as he was teaching, Pharisees and teachers of the law were sitting there, who had come from every village of Galilee and Judea and from Jerusalem. And the power of the Lord was with him to heal. 18 And behold, some men were bringing on a bed a man who was paralyzed, and they were seeking to bring him in and lay him before Jesus, 19 but finding no way to bring him in, because of the crowd, they went up on the roof and let him down with his bed through the tiles into the midst before Jesus. 20 And when he saw their faith, he said, "Man, your sins are forgiven you." 21 And the scribes and the Pharisees began to question, saying, "Who is this who speaks blasphemies? Who can forgive sins but God alone?" 22 When Jesus perceived their thoughts, he answered them, "Why do you question in your hearts? 23 Which is easier, to say, 'Your sins are forgiven you,' or to say, 'Rise and walk'? 24 But that you may know that the Son of Man has authority on earth to forgive sins"—he said to the man who was paralyzed—"I say to you, rise, pick up your bed and go home." 25 And immediately he rose up before them and picked up what he had been lying on and went home, glorifying

God. 26 And amazement seized them all, and they glorified God and were filled with awe, saying, "We have seen extraordinary things today."

1. For a Jewish person, having leprosy not only meant physical pain and sickness, it also meant that you were ceremonially unclean, and therefore cut off from God and his people. With this in mind, what is the full significance of Jesus' healing of the leper?

2. What is Jesus' priority for the paralyzed man?

3. How does Jesus demonstrate his authority to forgive sins?

PONDER What does Jesus' authority to forgive sins tell you about his identity?

PRAYER IDEAS Thank God that Jesus has the authority to cleanse the unclean and forgive sinners. Spend some time confessing your sins and asking the Lord Jesus to forgive you.

After this he went out and saw a tax collector named Levi, sitting at the tax booth. And he said to him, "Follow me." 28 And leaving everything, he rose and followed him.

29 And Levi made him a great feast in his house, and there was a large company of tax collectors and others reclining at table with them. 30 And the Pharisees and their scribes grumbled at his disciples, saying, "Why do you eat and drink with tax collectors and sinners?" 31 And Jesus answered them, "Those who are well have no need of a physician, but those who are sick. 32 I have not come to call the righteous but sinners to repentance."

33 And they said to him, "The disciples of John fast often and offer prayers, and so do the disciples of the Pharisees, but yours eat and drink." 34 And Jesus said to them, "Can you make wedding guests fast while the bridegroom is with them? 35 The days will come when the bridegroom is taken away from them, and then they will fast in those days." 36 He also told them a parable: "No one tears a piece from a new garment and puts it on an old garment. If he does, he will tear the new, and the piece from the new will not match the old. 37 And no one puts new wine into old wineskins. If he does, the new wine will burst the skins and it will be spilled, and the skins will be destroyed. 38 But new wine must be put into fresh wineskins. 39 And no one after drinking old wine desires new, for he says, 'The old is good.'"

1. Why are the Pharisees upset with Jesus (vv. 30, 33)?

2. What explanation does Jesus give for the type of company he keeps (v. 31)?

3. Why is it appropriate that Jesus' disciples don't fast (vv. 34-39)?

PONDER Jesus says he didn't come for "the righteous". Do you think that "the righteous" exist? Are you comfortable identifying yourself as a sick sinner in need of help?

PRAYER IDEAS Ask God to help you have a realistic view of yourself so that you see your need for Jesus.

On a Sabbath, while he was going through the grainfields, his disciples plucked and ate some heads of grain, rubbing them in their hands. 2 But some of the Pharisees said, "Why are you doing what is not lawful to do on the Sabbath?" 3 And Jesus answered them, "Have you not read what David did when he was hungry, he and those who were with him: 4 how he entered the house of God and took and ate the bread of the Presence, which is not lawful for any but the priests to eat, and also gave it to those with him?" 5 And he said to them, "The Son of Man is lord of the Sabbath."

6 On another Sabbath, he entered the synagogue and was teaching, and a man was

there whose right hand was withered. [7] And the scribes and the Pharisees watched him, to see whether he would heal on the Sabbath, so that they might find a reason to accuse him. [8] But he knew their thoughts, and he said to the man with the withered hand, "Come and stand here." And he rose and stood there. [9] And Jesus said to them, "I ask you, is it lawful on the Sabbath to do good or to do harm, to save life or to destroy it?" [10] And after looking around at them all he said to him, "Stretch out your hand." And he did so, and his hand was restored. [11] But they were filled with fury and discussed with one another what they might do to Jesus.

1. In verses 1-5, why are the Pharisees offended?

2. Jesus could argue with the Pharisees about their interpretation of what the law allows on the Sabbath, but he chooses to make a

bigger point instead. What is it?

3. What is new about the Pharisees' attitude in verse 7?

4. How does Jesus demonstrate the claim he made in verse 5?

PONDER Jesus claims to have the authority to say what the Old Testament law really means. What are the implications for the way Christians should apply the Old Testament law?

PRAYER IDEAS Ask God to help you to understand and apply his law in a way that recognizes Jesus' lordship.

READING 19   LUKE 6:12-26 █

In these days he went out to the mountain to pray, and all night he continued in prayer to God. [13] And when day came, he called his disciples and chose from them twelve, whom he named apostles: [14] Simon, whom he named Peter, and Andrew his brother, and James and John, and Philip, and Bartholomew, [15] and Matthew, and Thomas, and James the son of Alphaeus, and Simon who was called the Zealot, [16] and Judas the son of James, and Judas Iscariot, who became a traitor.

[17] And he came down with them and stood on a level place, with a great crowd of his disciples and a great multitude of people from all Judea and Jerusalem and the seacoast of Tyre and Sidon, [18] who came to hear him and to be healed of their diseases. And those who were troubled with unclean spirits were cured. [19] And all the crowd sought to touch him, for power came out from him and healed them all.

[20] And he lifted up his eyes on his disciples, and said:

"Blessed are you who are poor, for yours is the kingdom of God.

[21] "Blessed are you who are hungry now, for you shall be satisfied.

"Blessed are you who weep now, for you shall laugh.

[22] "Blessed are you when people hate you and when they exclude you and revile you and spurn your name as evil, on account of the Son of Man! [23] Rejoice in that day, and

leap for joy, for behold, your reward is great in heaven; for so their fathers did to the prophets.

²⁴ "But woe to you who are rich, for you have received your consolation.

²⁵ "Woe to you who are full now, for you shall be hungry.

"Woe to you who laugh now, for you shall mourn and weep.

²⁶ "Woe to you, when all people speak well of you, for so their fathers did to the false prophets."

1. According to Jesus, what kind of people are blessed?

2. How will the poor and hungry be blessed (cf. 1:53,[13] 4:18[14])?

3. What does Jesus say about those who are rich, full and laughing now?

PONDER What makes it difficult for Christians in the western world to see themselves as 'poor', 'hungry' and 'weeping'?

PRAYER IDEAS Ask God to make you 'poor' and 'hungry' enough to turn to Christ continually for salvation.

POINTER There have already been hints that sickness in Luke's Gospel is not only a physical problem but a spiritual problem (cf. 5:31).[15] Similarly, poverty, hunger and mourning express a spiritual state of complete helplessness and need (cf. Isa 61 and Ps 107 in the Appendix, pp. 68-70). It is these people who turn to Christ and receive blessing. In contrast, the rich, the full and the laughers view themselves as self-sufficient. They don't see their need, and so they fail to turn to Christ to receive his blessing.

READING 20   LUKE 6:27-49 ▮

"But I say to you who hear, Love your enemies, do good to those who hate you, ²⁸ bless those who curse you, pray for those who abuse you. ²⁹ To one who strikes you on the cheek, offer the other also, and from one who takes away your cloak do not withhold your tunic either. ³⁰ Give to everyone who begs from you, and from one who takes away your goods do not demand them back. ³¹ And as you wish that others would do to you, do so to them.

³² "If you love those who love you, what benefit is that to you? For even sinners love those who love them. ³³ And if you do good to those who do good to you, what benefit is that to you? For even sinners do the same. ³⁴ And if you lend to those from whom you expect to receive, what credit is that to you? Even sinners lend to sinners, to get back the same amount. ³⁵ But love your enemies, and do good, and lend, expecting nothing in return, and your reward will be great, and you will be sons of the Most High, for he is kind to the ungrateful and the evil. ³⁶ Be

---

13. "... he has filled the hungry with good things,
     and the rich he has sent away empty."
14. "The Spirit of the Lord is upon me,
     because he has anointed me
        to proclaim good news to the poor.

He has sent me to proclaim liberty to the captives
     and recovering of sight to the blind,
        to set at liberty those who are oppressed ..."
15. And Jesus answered them, "Those who are well have no need of a physician, but those who are sick."

merciful, even as your Father is merciful.

37 "Judge not, and you will not be judged; condemn not, and you will not be condemned; forgive, and you will be forgiven; 38 give, and it will be given to you. Good measure, pressed down, shaken together, running over, will be put into your lap. For with the measure you use it will be measured back to you."

39 He also told them a parable: "Can a blind man lead a blind man? Will they not both fall into a pit? 40 A disciple is not above his teacher, but everyone when he is fully trained will be like his teacher. 41 Why do you see the speck that is in your brother's eye, but do not notice the log that is in your own eye? 42 How can you say to your brother, 'Brother, let me take out the speck that is in your eye,' when you yourself do not see the log that is in your own eye? You hypocrite, first take the log out of your own eye, and then you will see clearly to take out the speck that is in your brother's eye.

43 "For no good tree bears bad fruit, nor again does a bad tree bear good fruit, 44 for each tree is known by its own fruit. For figs are not gathered from thornbushes, nor are grapes picked from a bramble bush. 45 The good person out of the good treasure of his heart produces good, and the evil person out of his evil treasure produces evil, for out of the abundance of the heart his mouth speaks.

46 "Why do you call me 'Lord, Lord,' and not do what I tell you? 47 Everyone who comes to me and hears my words and does them, I will show you what he is like: 48 he is like a man building a house, who dug deep and laid the foundation on the rock. And when a flood arose, the stream broke against that house and could not shake it, because it had been well built. 49 But the one who hears and does not do them is like a man who built a house on the ground without a foundation. When the stream broke against it, immediately it fell, and the ruin of that house was great."

1. How does Jesus re-interpret the command to love your neighbour?

2. What kind of judgement does Jesus forbid?

3. How does the parable of the builders (vv. 47-49) highlight the right way and the wrong way to respond to Jesus' teaching?

PONDER How has your study of Luke 1-6 increased your confidence in Jesus Christ?

PRAYER IDEAS Ask God to help you put Jesus' teaching into practice. Thank him for what you have learned about Jesus in Luke 1-6.

AMOS

INTRODUCTION

"The LORD roars from Zion ..." So begins the prophecy of Amos. Amos prophesied around 760 BC, a point in Israel's history when they were divided into a southern kingdom (Judah) and a northern kingdom (Israel). Amos comes from Tekoa in Judah in the south but prophesies to the Israelites in the north. The "roar" of God's voice begins with judgement on the surrounding nations (1:1-2:3) before focusing on God's people (2:4-9:10). It's sobering stuff, and it makes for an indispensable backdrop to the climactic word of hope at the end of the book (9:11-15).

You might like to use this prayer (or your own variation on it) before each of the next 20 studies:

Father in heaven,
You are the maker of all. You are the God who speaks and the earth withers. Keep me from hardening my heart to your word as Israel did. Help me to receive and treasure your word that, by it, I might live. In Jesus' name,
Amen.

READING 21   AMOS 1:1-2

The words of Amos, who was among the shepherds of Tekoa, which he saw concerning Israel in the days of Uzziah king of Judah and in the days of Jeroboam the son of Joash, king of Israel, two years before the earthquake.

² And he said:

"The LORD roars from Zion
    and utters his voice from Jerusalem;
the pastures of the shepherds mourn,
    and the top of Carmel withers."

1. What do you think it means when it says that Amos "saw" these words from God?

2. What does the word "roars" imply about who God is and why he is speaking?

3. Why do you think the pastures and Mount Carmel respond to God's voice in this way?

PONDER It is both a wonderful privilege and a disturbing experience to hear God speak. Read Hebrews 1:1-4.[16] When you hear God's voice through his Son, are you thankful? Do you take what he says seriously?

PRAYER IDEAS Thank God for speaking to you through Jesus in a way that is even clearer than when he spoke through Amos. Ask him to help you to always treat his word with serious respect.

READING 22   AMOS 1:3-8

Thus says the LORD:

"For three transgressions of Damascus,
    and for four, I will not revoke the
        punishment,
because they have threshed Gilead
    with threshing sledges of iron.
⁴ So I will send a fire upon the house of
      Hazael,
    and it shall devour the strongholds of
      Ben-hadad.
⁵ I will break the gate-bar of Damascus,
    and cut off the inhabitants from the
      Valley of Aven,
and him who holds the scepter from
      Beth-eden;
and the people of Syria shall go into
    exile to Kir,"
                says the LORD.

⁶ Thus says the LORD:

"For three transgressions of Gaza,
    and for four, I will not revoke the
        punishment,
because they carried into exile a whole
      people
to deliver them up to Edom.
⁷ So I will send a fire upon the wall of Gaza,

and it shall devour her strongholds.
⁸ I will cut off the inhabitants from Ashdod,
    and him who holds the scepter from
      Ashkelon;
I will turn my hand against Ekron,
    and the remnant of the Philistines shall
      perish,"
              says the Lord GOD.

1. These are the first two in a series of judgements against Israel's neighbours—in this case, Damascus (vv. 3-5) and Gaza (vv. 6-8). What are their sins?

2. What will God do when he judges them?

PONDER The day when God will judge the whole earth through Jesus is coming (Acts 17:29-31).[17] How does knowing this affect how you live your life now?

---

16. Long ago, at many times and in many ways, God spoke to our fathers by the prophets, ² but in these last days he has spoken to us by his Son, whom he appointed the heir of all things, through whom also he created the world. ³ He is the radiance of the glory of God and the exact imprint of his nature, and he upholds the universe by the word of his power. After making purification for sins, he sat down at the right hand of the Majesty on high, ⁴ having become as much superior to angels as the name he has inherited is more

excellent than theirs.
17. "Being then God's offspring, we ought not to think that the divine being is like gold or silver or stone, an image formed by the art and imagination of man. ³⁰ The times of ignorance God overlooked, but now he commands all people everywhere to repent, ³¹ because he has fixed a day on which he will judge the world in righteousness by a man whom he has appointed; and of this he has given assurance to all by raising him from the dead."

PRAYER IDEAS Ask God to help all people around the world to recognize that judgement is coming.

POINTER v. 4: For a better idea of who King Hazael was and what he did, read 2 Kings 8:7-15 (see the Appendix, p. 70), 10:32-33,[18] 13:3,[19] 7[20] and 22.[21]

READING 23   AMOS 1:9-12

Thus says the LORD:

"For three transgressions of Tyre,
    and for four, I will not revoke the
        punishment,
because they delivered up a whole people
    to Edom,
    and did not remember the covenant of
        brotherhood.
[10] So I will send a fire upon the wall of Tyre,
    and it shall devour her strongholds."

[11] Thus says the LORD:

"For three transgressions of Edom,
    and for four, I will not revoke the
        punishment,
because he pursued his brother with the sword
    and cast off all pity,
and his anger tore perpetually,
    and he kept his wrath forever.
[12] So I will send a fire upon Teman,
    and it shall devour the strongholds of
        Bozrah."

1. These are the next two judgement speeches—against Tyre (vv. 9-10) and Edom (vv. 11-12). How have they both sinned against their 'brother' (vv. 9, 11)?

2. What will God do when he judges them?

PONDER As a Christian, you are part of a 'brotherhood' of believers (1 Pet 2:17).[22] What kind of privileges and obligations does this bring?

PRAYER IDEAS Praise God that, despite your natural inclination to sin against others, Jesus is the head of a new family of love to which you belong. Ask God to help you to love the brothers and sisters in your spiritual family.

POINTER v. 11: The Edomites were the descendants of Esau, the brother of Jacob (Gen 25:21-26).[23] The Israelites were Jacob's descendants. That makes Israel the 'brother' of Edom.

---

18. In those days the LORD began to cut off parts of Israel. Hazael defeated them throughout the territory of Israel: [33] from the Jordan eastward, all the land of Gilead, the Gadites, and the Reubenites, and the Manassites, from Aroer, which is by the Valley of the Arnon, that is, Gilead and Bashan.
19. And the anger of the LORD was kindled against Israel, and he gave them continually into the hand of Hazael king of Syria and into the hand of Ben-hadad the son of Hazael.
20. For there was not left to Jehoahaz an army of more than fifty horsemen and ten chariots and ten thousand footmen, for the king of Syria had destroyed them and made them like the dust at threshing.
21. Now Hazael king of Syria oppressed Israel all the days of Jehoahaz.
22. Honor everyone. Love the brotherhood. Fear God. Honor the emperor.

23. And Isaac prayed to the LORD for his wife, because she was barren. And the LORD granted his prayer, and Rebekah his wife conceived. [22] The children struggled together within her, and she said, "If it is thus, why is this happening to me?" So she went to inquire of the LORD. [23] And the LORD said to her,

"Two nations are in your womb,
    and two peoples from within you shall be divided;
the one shall be stronger than the other,
    the older shall serve the younger."

[24] When her days to give birth were completed, behold, there were twins in her womb. [25] The first came out red, all his body like a hairy cloak, so they called his name Esau. [26] Afterward his brother came out with his hand holding Esau's heel, so his name was called Jacob. Isaac was sixty years old when she bore them.

Thus says the LORD:

"For three transgressions of the Ammonites,
    and for four, I will not revoke the
        punishment,
because they have ripped open pregnant
        women in Gilead,
    that they might enlarge their border.
14 So I will kindle a fire in the wall of
        Rabbah,
    and it shall devour her strongholds,
with shouting on the day of battle,
    with a tempest in the day of the
        whirlwind;
15 and their king shall go into exile,
    he and his princes together,"
                        says the LORD.

2:1 Thus says the LORD:

"For three transgressions of Moab,
    and for four, I will not revoke the
        punishment,
because he burned to lime
    the bones of the king of Edom.
2 So I will send a fire upon Moab,
    and it shall devour the strongholds of
        Kerioth,
and Moab shall die amid uproar,
    amid shouting and the sound of the
        trumpet;
3 I will cut off the ruler from its midst,
    and will kill all its princes with him,"
                        says the LORD.

1. These are the next two judgement
speeches—against Ammon (1:13-15) and
Moab (2:1-3). How have they both shown
cruelty to the helpless?

2. What will God do when he judges them?

PONDER Read back over 1:4,[24] 7,[25] 10,[26] 12,[27]
14 and 2:2. What do these verses tell you
about who God is? What do they tell you
about the nature of his wrath?

PRAYER IDEAS Read 2 Thessalonians 1:5-10[28]
and reflect on the 'fire' of God's wrath that
is still to come. Thank him for rescuing you
from that fire, and ask him to work in the
people you know who don't currently submit
to the gospel of Jesus so that they will turn
and obey him.

---

24. "So I will send a fire upon the house of Hazael,
    and it shall devour the strongholds of Ben-hadad."
25. "So I will send a fire upon the wall of Gaza,
    and it shall devour her strongholds."
26. "So I will send a fire upon the wall of Tyre,
    and it shall devour her strongholds."
27. "So I will send a fire upon Teman,
    and it shall devour the strongholds of Bozrah."
28. This is evidence of the righteous judgment of God, that
you may be considered worthy of the kingdom of God, for
which you are also suffering— 6 since indeed God considers

it just to repay with affliction those who afflict you, 7 and to
grant relief to you who are afflicted as well as to us, when the
Lord Jesus is revealed from heaven with his mighty angels 8 in
flaming fire, inflicting vengeance on those who do not know
God and on those who do not obey the gospel of our Lord
Jesus. 9 They will suffer the punishment of eternal destruction,
away from the presence of the Lord and from the glory of
his might, 10 when he comes on that day to be glorified in his
saints, and to be marveled at among all who have believed,
because our testimony to you was believed.

Thus says the LORD:

"For three transgressions of Judah,
    and for four, I will not revoke the
        punishment,
because they have rejected the law of the
      LORD,
    and have not kept his statutes,
but their lies have led them astray,
    those after which their fathers walked.
5 So I will send a fire upon Judah,
    and it shall devour the strongholds of
      Jerusalem."

*1. This final judgement speech against Judah
is, in some ways, the same as the others.
However, it is also different because, like
Israel, the people of Judah are part of
God's chosen people. How are the sins
they've committed different from the sins
of the other nations?*

*2. Is God any less angry with his own people
than with the other nations?*

PONDER Read James 1:22-25.[29] How can
you avoid the mistakes the people of the Old
Testament made?

PRAYER IDEAS Ask God to forgive you for
the times when you are careless and lazy in
your approach to his word. Ask him to help
you never to reject his word but, instead, to
meditate on it and obey it.

Thus says the LORD:

"For three transgressions of Israel,
    and for four, I will not revoke the
        punishment,
because they sell the righteous for silver,
    and the needy for a pair of sandals—
7 those who trample the head of the poor
      into the dust of the earth
    and turn aside the way of the afflicted;

a man and his father go in to the same girl,
    so that my holy name is profaned;
8 they lay themselves down beside every
      altar
    on garments taken in pledge,
and in the house of their God they drink
    the wine of those who have been fined.

9 "Yet it was I who destroyed the Amorite
    before them,

---

29. But be doers of the word, and not hearers only, deceiving
yourselves. 23 For if anyone is a hearer of the word and not a
doer, he is like a man who looks intently at his natural face
in a mirror. 24 For he looks at himself and goes away and at
once forgets what he was like. 25 But the one who looks into
the perfect law, the law of liberty, and perseveres, being no
hearer who forgets but a doer who acts, he will be blessed in
his doing.

whose height was like the height of the
    cedars
and who was as strong as the oaks;
I destroyed his fruit above
    and his roots beneath.
¹⁰ Also it was I who brought you up out of
    the land of Egypt
and led you forty years in the
    wilderness,
to possess the land of the Amorite.
¹¹ And I raised up some of your sons for
    prophets,
and some of your young men for
    Nazirites.
Is it not indeed so, O people of Israel?"
                 declares the LORD.

¹² "But you made the Nazirites drink wine,
    and commanded the prophets,
saying, 'You shall not prophesy.'"

1. *What are the sins of God's people (vv. 6-8,
12)?*

2. *How has God been kind to his people
(vv. 9-11)?*

PONDER Privilege brings responsibility.
The Israelites may have thought that the
privilege of being God's people meant they
could behave in any way they chose, but God
is reminding them here that this is not the
case. Paul corrects a similar misunderstanding
in Romans 6:1-4.[30] In what areas are you
tempted to continue sinning?

PRAYER IDEAS Ask God to strengthen you
so that you are not a complacent Christian
but instead one who walks in the "newness
of life" you have in Jesus.

POINTERS v. 8: "garments taken in pledge"
seems to refer to the misuse of things
possessed because of debt or crime (see Exod
22:25-27[31] and Deut 24:12-13[32]).
    vv. 11-12: The Nazirites were Israelites
who had taken special vows of devotion to
God (see Numbers 6:1-18 in the Appendix,
pp. 70-71).

---

⁹ "Yet it was I who destroyed the Amorite
    before them,
whose height was like the height of the
    cedars
and who was as strong as the oaks;

I destroyed his fruit above
    and his roots beneath.
¹⁰ Also it was I who brought you up out of
    the land of Egypt
and led you forty years in the wilderness,

---

30. What shall we say then? Are we to continue in sin that
grace may abound? ² By no means! How can we who died to
sin still live in it? ³ Do you not know that all of us who have
been baptized into Christ Jesus were baptized into his death?
⁴ We were buried therefore with him by baptism into death, in
order that, just as Christ was raised from the dead by the glory
of the Father, we too might walk in newness of life.
31. "If you lend money to any of my people with you who is
poor, you shall not be like a moneylender to him, and you shall

not exact interest from him. ²⁶ If ever you take your neighbor's
cloak in pledge, you shall return it to him before the sun goes
down, ²⁷ for that is his only covering, and it is his cloak for his
body; in what else shall he sleep? And if he cries to me, I will
hear, for I am compassionate."
32. "And if he is a poor man, you shall not sleep in his
pledge. ¹³ You shall restore to him the pledge as the sun sets,
that he may sleep in his cloak and bless you. And it shall be
righteousness for you before the LORD your God."

to possess the land of the Amorite.
¹¹ And I raised up some of your sons for
    prophets,
and some of your young men for
    Nazirites.
Is it not indeed so, O people of Israel?"
                          declares the Lord.

¹² "But you made the Nazirites drink wine,
    and commanded the prophets,
    saying, 'You shall not prophesy.'

¹³ "Behold, I will press you down in your
    place,
    as a cart full of sheaves presses down.
¹⁴ Flight shall perish from the swift,
    and the strong shall not retain his
       strength,
    nor shall the mighty save his life;
¹⁵ he who handles the bow shall not stand,
    and he who is swift of foot shall not
       save himself,
    nor shall he who rides the horse save
       his life;
¹⁶ and he who is stout of heart among the
    mighty
    shall flee away naked in that day,"
                          declares the Lord.

1. What has God done for his people? (Refer
   back to your answers in Reading 26.)

2. What does God say he is going to do now?

3. Will anyone escape from God's
   punishment?

PONDER Israel may have rejoiced upon
hearing God's judgements upon their
neighbours, but now they have to face
the fact that they're under the same
condemnation. Read 2 Corinthians 5:10.[33]
Have you ever been tempted to think that
because you are one of God's people, you will
never be accountable before God?

PRAYER IDEAS Ask God to help you live
a life so glorifying to him that he will
commend you on that final day.

LUKE 1-6

READING 28   AMOS 3:1-8

Hear this word that the Lord has spoken
against you, O people of Israel, against
the whole family that I brought up out of the
land of Egypt:

² "You only have I known
    of all the families of the earth;
therefore I will punish you
    for all your iniquities.

³ "Do two walk together,
    unless they have agreed to meet?
⁴ Does a lion roar in the forest,
    when he has no prey?
Does a young lion cry out from his den,
    if he has taken nothing?
⁵ Does a bird fall in a snare on the earth,
    when there is no trap for it?
Does a snare spring up from the ground,
    when it has taken nothing?

2 CORINTHIANS

---

33. For we must all appear before the judgment seat of Christ,
so that each one may receive what is due for what he has done
in the body, whether good or evil.

⁶ Is a trumpet blown in a city,
  and the people are not afraid?
Does disaster come to a city,
  unless the Lᴏʀᴅ has done it?

⁷ "For the Lord Gᴏᴅ does nothing
  without revealing his secret
  to his servants the prophets.
⁸ The lion has roared;
  who will not fear?
The Lord Gᴏᴅ has spoken;
  who can but prophesy?"

1. What is tragic about verses 1-2?

3. If the answer to the two questions in verse 6 is 'No', what is Amos saying?

4. If God 'roars' (cf. 1:2),³⁴ what must Amos do? How should his people respond to him?

2. What is the answer to all of the rhetorical questions in verses 3-5?

PONDER Read Revelation 14:6-7.³⁵ How is the Christian gospel a gospel about fearing God? Is it the same kind of 'fear' Amos is talking about here?

PRAYER IDEAS Ask God to lead you to glorify and worship him with your whole life. Ask him to cause others to fear him too.

READING 29 AMOS 3:9-15

Proclaim to the strongholds in Ashdod
  and to the strongholds in the land of
  Egypt,
and say, "Assemble yourselves on the
  mountains of Samaria,
  and see the great tumults within her,
  and the oppressed in her midst."

¹⁰ "They do not know how to do right,"
  declares the Lᴏʀᴅ,
"those who store up violence and
  robbery in their strongholds."

¹¹ Therefore thus says the Lord Gᴏᴅ:

---

34. And he said:

"The Lᴏʀᴅ roars from Zion
  and utters his voice from Jerusalem;
the pastures of the shepherds mourn,
  and the top of Carmel withers."

35. Then I saw another angel flying directly overhead, with an eternal gospel to proclaim to those who dwell on earth, to every nation and tribe and language and people. ⁷ And he said with a loud voice, "Fear God and give him glory, because the hour of his judgment has come, and worship him who made heaven and earth, the sea and the springs of water."

"An adversary shall surround the land
and bring down your defenses from you,
and your strongholds shall be
plundered."

¹² Thus says the LORD: "As the shepherd rescues from the mouth of the lion two legs, or a piece of an ear, so shall the people of Israel who dwell in Samaria be rescued, with the corner of a couch and part of a bed.

¹³ "Hear, and testify against the house of
Jacob,"
declares the Lord GOD, the God of hosts,
¹⁴ "that on the day I punish Israel for his
transgressions,
I will punish the altars of Bethel,
and the horns of the altar shall be cut off
and fall to the ground.
¹⁵ I will strike the winter house along with
the summer house,
and the houses of ivory shall perish,
and the great houses shall come to an end,"
declares the LORD.

1. What are the sins of Israel according to verses 9-10?

2. How will God punish Israel (vv. 11-15)?

3. Does verse 12 hold out much hope for Israel, or is the word "rescued" ironic?

PONDER Is there any way for Israel to avoid God's punishment? Read 1 Thessalonians 5:9-10.³⁶ Is there any way for us to escape God's wrath?

PRAYER IDEAS Thank God that you don't have to face the day of his wrath without hope. Praise him for destining you for salvation instead of wrath.

POINTERS v. 9: Ashdod (which lies in Philistia—cf. 1:8)³⁷ and Egypt are two of Israel's neighbours. Here they are called to be witnesses of Israel's sin, which would have been greatly humiliating for God's people.
v. 12: If a sheep is taken by a lion and all that's left when the shepherd finds it is two legs or a piece of an ear, what the shepherd 'rescues' are merely signs that the sheep has been destroyed.

---

36. For God has not destined us for wrath, but to obtain salvation through our Lord Jesus Christ, ¹⁰ who died for us so that whether we are awake or asleep we might live with him.
37. "I will cut off the inhabitants from Ashdod,

and him who holds the scepter from Ashkelon;
I will turn my hand against Ekron,
and the remnant of the Philistines shall perish,"
says the Lord GOD.

1 "Hear this word, you cows of Bashan,
who are on the mountain of Samaria,
who oppress the poor, who crush the needy,
who say to your husbands, 'Bring, that
we may drink!'
² The Lord God has sworn by his holiness
that, behold, the days are coming upon
you,
when they shall take you away with hooks,
even the last of you with fishhooks.
³ And you shall go out through the breaches,
each one straight ahead;
and you shall be cast out into Harmon,"
declares the Lord.

⁴ "Come to Bethel, and transgress;
to Gilgal, and multiply transgression;
bring your sacrifices every morning,
your tithes every three days;
⁵ offer a sacrifice of thanksgiving of that
which is leavened,
and proclaim freewill offerings, publish
them;
for so you love to do, O people of Israel!"
declares the Lord God.

*1. Who is God addressing in verses 1-3?
(Hint: they have "husbands".) Where are
they from?*

*2. Why does God swear "by his holiness"
(v. 2)?*

*3. Bethel and Gilgal were religious sites—
places of worship. Why does God call
these "cows of Bashan" to "transgress"
(i.e. sin) there rather than to worship
there?*

PONDER Amos is addressing Israelites who
are doing 'religious' things but whose hearts
are actually far from God. Read Matthew
6:1-6.**³⁸** Is this ever true of you?

PRAYER IDEAS Ask God to help you to steer
clear of 'religious' things that are purely
for show. Confess the ways in which you
sometimes fail him in this regard.

POINTER v. 4: Shrines in places like Bethel
and Gilgal were usually offensive to God
to begin with. Bethel, for example, was
originally set up as an alternative to the
place of worship that God had established in
Jerusalem (see 1 Kgs 12:25-30).**³⁹**

---

38. "Beware of practicing your righteousness before other people in order to be seen by them, for then you will have no reward from your Father who is in heaven.
² "Thus, when you give to the needy, sound no trumpet before you, as the hypocrites do in the synagogues and in the streets, that they may be praised by others. Truly, I say to you, they have received their reward. ³ But when you give to the needy, do not let your left hand know what your right hand is doing, ⁴ so that your giving may be in secret. And your Father who sees in secret will reward you.
⁵ "And when you pray, you must not be like the hypocrites. For they love to stand and pray in the synagogues and at the street corners, that they may be seen by others. Truly, I say to you, they have received their reward. ⁶ But when you pray, go into your room and shut the door and pray to your Father who

is in secret. And your Father who sees in secret will reward you."
39. Then Jeroboam built Shechem in the hill country of Ephraim and lived there. And he went out from there and built Penuel. ²⁶ And Jeroboam said in his heart, "Now the kingdom will turn back to the house of David. ²⁷ If this people go up to offer sacrifices in the temple of the Lord at Jerusalem, then the heart of this people will turn again to their lord, to Rehoboam king of Judah, and they will kill me and return to Rehoboam king of Judah." ²⁸ So the king took counsel and made two calves of gold. And he said to the people, "You have gone up to Jerusalem long enough. Behold your gods, O Israel, who brought you up out of the land of Egypt." ²⁹ And he set one in Bethel, and the other he put in Dan. ³⁰ Then this thing became a sin, for the people went as far as Dan to be before one.

6 I gave you cleanness of teeth in all your cities,
    and lack of bread in all your places,
yet you did not return to me,"
                                        declares the LORD.

7 "I also withheld the rain from you
    when there were yet three months to
        the harvest;
I would send rain on one city,
    and send no rain on another city;
one field would have rain,
    and the field on which it did not rain
        would wither;
8 so two or three cities would wander to
        another city
    to drink water, and would not be
        satisfied;
yet you did not return to me,"
                                        declares the LORD.

9 "I struck you with blight and mildew;
    your many gardens and your vineyards,
    your fig trees and your olive trees the
        locust devoured;
yet you did not return to me,"
                                        declares the LORD.

10 "I sent among you a pestilence after the
        manner of Egypt;
    I killed your young men with the
        sword,
and carried away your horses,
    and I made the stench of your camp go
        up into your nostrils;
yet you did not return to me,"
                                        declares the LORD.

11 "I overthrew some of you,
    as when God overthrew Sodom and
        Gomorrah,
    and you were as a brand plucked out of
        the burning;

yet you did not return to me,"
                                        declares the LORD.

12 "Therefore thus I will do to you, O Israel;
    because I will do this to you,
    prepare to meet your God, O Israel!"

13 For behold, he who forms the mountains
        and creates the wind,
    and declares to man what is his
        thought,
who makes the morning darkness,
    and treads on the heights of the earth—
    the LORD, the God of hosts, is his name!"

*1. Why do you think God sends all these
    disasters upon his people?*

*2. Why might God have continued to send
    these disasters, even after his people
    refused to return?*

*3. Why did they need to "prepare" to meet
    God (vv. 12-13)?*

LUKE 1-6

AMOS

2 CORINTHIANS

PONDER Throughout these painful experiences, God was patiently disciplining his people. Read Hebrews 12:4-11.[40] How has God used the painful experiences in your life to discipline you?

PRAYER IDEAS Thank God for his good purposes which hold true even in the midst of pain. Ask him to strengthen you to keep the end in view when the hard times come. Praise him using the words of Amos 4:13.

READING 32   AMOS 5:1-9 ▮

Hear this word that I take up over you in lamentation, O house of Israel:

2 "Fallen, no more to rise,
    is the virgin Israel;
forsaken on her land,
    with none to raise her up."

3 For thus says the Lord GOD:

"The city that went out a thousand
    shall have a hundred left,
and that which went out a hundred
    shall have ten left
to the house of Israel."

4 For thus says the LORD to the house of Israel:

"Seek me and live;
    5 but do not seek Bethel,
and do not enter into Gilgal
    or cross over to Beersheba;
for Gilgal shall surely go into exile,
    and Bethel shall come to nothing."

6 Seek the LORD and live,
    lest he break out like fire in the house
        of Joseph,

and it devour, with none to quench it
        for Bethel,
7 O you who turn justice to wormwood
    and cast down righteousness to the
        earth!

8 He who made the Pleiades and Orion,
    and turns deep darkness into the
        morning
    and darkens the day into night,
who calls for the waters of the sea
    and pours them out on the surface of
        the earth,
    the LORD is his name;
9 who makes destruction flash forth against
        the strong,
    so that destruction comes upon the
        fortress.

*1. Why is a "lamentation" over Israel
    appropriate?*

---

40. In your struggle against sin you have not yet resisted to the point of shedding your blood. 5 And have you forgotten the exhortation that addresses you as sons?

"My son, do not regard lightly the discipline of the Lord,
    nor be weary when reproved by him.
6 For the Lord disciplines the one he loves,
    and chastises every son whom he receives."

7 It is for discipline that you have to endure. God is treating you as sons. For what son is there whom his father does not discipline? 8 If you are left without discipline, in which all have participated, then you are illegitimate children and not sons. 9 Besides this, we have had earthly fathers who disciplined us and we respected them. Shall we not much more be subject to the Father of spirits and live? 10 For they disciplined us for a short time as it seemed best to them, but he disciplines us for our good, that we may share his holiness. 11 For the moment all discipline seems painful rather than pleasant, but later it yields the peaceful fruit of righteousness to those who have been trained by it.

2. Why should the people seek the Lord rather than their religious places?

PONDER What did Israel need to do in order to live (i.e. be spared from God's wrath)? Reflect on Jesus' words in John 11:25-26.[41] What do we need to do in order to live?

3. What do verses 8-9 tell you about God?

PRAYER IDEAS Praise God for being a God who both creates and destroys (vv. 8-9). Thank him for granting you eternal life through Jesus.

READING 33   AMOS 5:10-17

They hate him who reproves in the gate,
  and they abhor him who speaks the
        truth.
[11] Therefore because you trample on the poor
  and you exact taxes of grain from him,
you have built houses of hewn stone,
  but you shall not dwell in them;
you have planted pleasant vineyards,
  but you shall not drink their wine.
[12] For I know how many are your
        transgressions
  and how great are your sins—
you who afflict the righteous, who take a
        bribe,
  and turn aside the needy in the gate.
[13] Therefore he who is prudent will keep
        silent in such a time,
  for it is an evil time.

[14] Seek good, and not evil,
    that you may live;
and so the Lord, the God of hosts, will be
        with you,
    as you have said.

[15] Hate evil, and love good,
    and establish justice in the gate;
it may be that the Lord, the God of hosts,
    will be gracious to the remnant of Joseph.

[16] Therefore thus says the Lord, the God of hosts, the Lord:

"In all the squares there shall be wailing,
    and in all the streets they shall say,
        'Alas! Alas!'
They shall call the farmers to mourning
    and to wailing those who are skilled in
        lamentation,
[17] and in all vineyards there shall be wailing,
    for I will pass through your midst,"
                    says the Lord.

1. How do verses 14-15 spell out what it means to "seek the Lord" (5:6)?[42]

---

41. Jesus said to her, "I am the resurrection and the life. Whoever believes in me, though he die, yet shall he live, [26] and everyone who lives and believes in me shall never die. Do you believe this?"

42. "Seek the Lord and live,
    lest he break out like fire in the house of Joseph,
    and it devour, with none to quench it for Bethel ..."

2. What are the 'evils' the Israelites are to hate?

PONDER Seeking after God involves a new way of life—a life that hates evil and loves good. Read Romans 12:9-21 in the Appendix (p. 71). Is your life marked by this kind of hatred and love?

3. Is it significant that verse 15 says that God "may" be gracious?

PRAYER IDEAS Ask God to help you become more and more like a person who loves good and hates evil.

READING 34   AMOS 5:18-27

Woe to you who desire the day of the LORD!
  Why would you have the day of the LORD?
It is darkness, and not light,
  ¹⁹ as if a man fled from a lion,
  and a bear met him,
or went into the house and leaned his hand against the wall,
  and a serpent bit him.
²⁰ Is not the day of the LORD darkness, and not light,
  and gloom with no brightness in it?

²¹ "I hate, I despise your feasts,
  and I take no delight in your solemn assemblies.
²² Even though you offer me your burnt offerings and grain offerings,
  I will not accept them;
and the peace offerings of your fattened animals,
  I will not look upon them.
²³ Take away from me the noise of your songs;
  to the melody of your harps I will not listen.
²⁴ But let justice roll down like waters,
  and righteousness like an ever-flowing stream."

²⁵ "Did you bring to me sacrifices and offerings during the forty years in the wilderness, O house of Israel? ²⁶ You shall take up Sikkuth your king, and Kiyyun your star-god—your images that you made for yourselves, ²⁷ and I will send you into exile beyond Damascus," says the LORD, whose name is the God of hosts.

1. Why might the Israelites be 'desiring' the day of the Lord?

2. What does God say that day will actually be like for them?

3. How does God treat them in his anger?

PONDER Amos rebuked people who looked forward to the day of God's coming but who shouldn't have. Read 2 Peter 3:8-13.[43] What should be our attitude to the day of Lord? Why?

PRAYER IDEAS Praise God that, in his justice, there is a "day of the LORD" still to come. Thank him for what he has in store on that day. Ask him to help you live a holy and godly life while you wait.

READING 35   AMOS 6:1-14

1 "Woe to those who are at ease in Zion,
and to those who feel secure on the
mountain of Samaria,
the notable men of the first of the nations,
to whom the house of Israel comes!
2 Pass over to Calneh, and see,
and from there go to Hamath the great;
then go down to Gath of the Philistines.
Are you better than these kingdoms?
Or is their territory greater than your
territory,
3 O you who put far away the day of
disaster
and bring near the seat of violence?

4 "Woe to those who lie on beds of ivory
and stretch themselves out on their
couches,
and eat lambs from the flock
and calves from the midst of the stall,
5 who sing idle songs to the sound of the
harp
and like David invent for themselves
instruments of music,
6 who drink wine in bowls
and anoint themselves with the finest
oils,
but are not grieved over the ruin of
Joseph!

7 Therefore they shall now be the first of
those who go into exile,
and the revelry of those who stretch
themselves out shall pass away."

8 The Lord GOD has sworn by himself, declares the LORD, the God of hosts:

"I abhor the pride of Jacob
and hate his strongholds,
and I will deliver up the city and all that
is in it."

9 And if ten men remain in one house, they shall die. 10 And when one's relative, the one who anoints him for burial, shall take him up to bring the bones out of the house, and shall say to him who is in the innermost parts of the house, "Is there still anyone with you?" he shall say, "No"; and he shall say, "Silence! We must not mention the name of the LORD."

11 For behold, the LORD commands,
and the great house shall be struck
down into fragments,
and the little house into bits.
12 Do horses run on rocks?
Does one plow there with oxen?
But you have turned justice into poison

---

43. But do not overlook this one fact, beloved, that with the Lord one day is as a thousand years, and a thousand years as one day. 9 The Lord is not slow to fulfill his promise as some count slowness, but is patient toward you, not wishing that any should perish, but that all should reach repentance. 10 But the day of the Lord will come like a thief, and then the heavens will pass away with a roar, and the heavenly bodies will be burned up and dissolved, and the earth and the works that are done on it will be exposed.
11 Since all these things are thus to be dissolved, what sort of people ought you to be in lives of holiness and godliness, 12 waiting for and hastening the coming of the day of God, because of which the heavens will be set on fire and dissolved, and the heavenly bodies will melt as they burn! 13 But according to his promise we are waiting for new heavens and a new earth in which righteousness dwells.

and the fruit of righteousness into
  wormwood—
13 you who rejoice in Lo-debar,
  who say, "Have we not by our own
    strength
  captured Karnaim for ourselves?"
14 "For behold, I will raise up against you a
    nation,
  O house of Israel," declares the Lord, the
    God of hosts;
"and they shall oppress you from Lebo-
    hamath
  to the Brook of the Arabah."

1. *Perhaps as a parallel to 4:1-3,*[44] *which
   addresses the wealthy women of
   Samaria, Amos addresses the "notable"
   men of Samaria in verses 1-7. What are
   their sins?*

2. *How will God judge Israel in verses 9-14?*

3. *How is verse 8 a summary of the whole
   chapter?*

PONDER God was angry with Israel because
of their pride and because they had run after
the things of the world. Read James 4:4-10[45]
and notice how James also connects pride
and "friendship with the world". What are
Christians to do instead?

PRAYER IDEAS Ask God to help you to
always be humble, drawing near to God,
resisting the devil and purifying your heart.

POINTER v. 2: Calneh, Hamath and Gath
were cities in the nations surrounding Israel.

READING 36   AMOS 7:1-9

This is what the Lord God showed me:
  behold, he was forming locusts when the
latter growth was just beginning to sprout,
and behold, it was the latter growth after
the king's mowings. 2 When they had finished
eating the grass of the land, I said,

  "O Lord God, please forgive!
    How can Jacob stand?

  He is so small!"
3 The Lord relented concerning this:
  "It shall not be," said the Lord.

  4 This is what the Lord God showed me:
behold, the Lord God was calling for a
judgment by fire, and it devoured the great
deep and was eating up the land. 5 Then I said,

---

44. "Hear this word, you cows of Bashan,
    who are on the mountain of Samaria,
who oppress the poor, who crush the needy,
    who say to your husbands, 'Bring, that we may drink!'
2 The Lord God has sworn by his holiness
    that, behold, the days are coming upon you,
when they shall take you away with hooks,
    even the last of you with fishhooks.
3 And you shall go out through the breaches,
    each one straight ahead;
    and you shall be cast out into Harmon,"
                                    declares the Lord.

45. You adulterous people! Do you not know that friendship
with the world is enmity with God? Therefore whoever wishes
to be a friend of the world makes himself an enemy of God.
5 Or do you suppose it is to no purpose that the Scripture
says, "He yearns jealously over the spirit that he has made to
dwell in us"? 6 But he gives more grace. Therefore it says, "God
opposes the proud, but gives grace to the humble." 7 Submit
yourselves therefore to God. Resist the devil, and he will flee
from you. 8 Draw near to God, and he will draw near to you.
Cleanse your hands, you sinners, and purify your hearts, you
double-minded. 9 Be wretched and mourn and weep. Let your
laughter be turned to mourning and your joy to gloom. 10 Humble
yourselves before the Lord, and he will exalt you.

"O Lord God, please cease!
How can Jacob stand?
He is so small!"
⁶ The Lord relented concerning this:
"This also shall not be," said the Lord God.

⁷ This is what he showed me: behold, the Lord was standing beside a wall built with a plumb line, with a plumb line in his hand. ⁸ And the Lord said to me, "Amos, what do you see?" And I said, "A plumb line." Then the Lord said,

"Behold, I am setting a plumb line
in the midst of my people Israel;
I will never again pass by them;
⁹ the high places of Isaac shall be made
desolate,
and the sanctuaries of Israel shall be
laid waste,
and I will rise against the house of
Jeroboam with the sword."

1. What leads God to relent after the first two visions?

2. What does the third vision reveal about Israel?

3. What does this section reveal about Amos' authority to speak on God's behalf?

PONDER Ultimately, God's judgement is unavoidable (vv. 7-9). However, he is quick to be merciful in response to the prayers of his people (vv. 1-6). Do you sometimes fail to receive mercy from God because you fail to ask (Jas 4:2)?[46]

PRAYER IDEAS Ask God to be merciful towards those you know and love who are still outside his kingdom.

POINTER v. 7: A plumb line is a building tool that helps the builder test whether a wall is being built straight.

READING 37   AMOS 7:10-17

Then Amaziah the priest of Bethel sent to Jeroboam king of Israel, saying, "Amos has conspired against you in the midst of the house of Israel. The land is not able to bear all his words. ¹¹ For thus Amos has said,

"'Jeroboam shall die by the sword,
and Israel must go into exile
away from his land.'"

¹² And Amaziah said to Amos, "O seer, go, flee away to the land of Judah, and eat bread there, and prophesy there, ¹³ but never again prophesy at Bethel, for it is the king's sanctuary, and it is a temple of the kingdom." ¹⁴ Then Amos answered and said to Amaziah, "I was no prophet, nor a prophet's son, but I was a herdsman and a dresser of sycamore figs. ¹⁵ But the Lord took me from following the flock, and the Lord said to me,

---

46. You desire and do not have, so you murder. You covet and cannot obtain, so you fight and quarrel. You do not have, because you do not ask.

'Go, prophesy to my people Israel.' ¹⁶ Now therefore hear the word of the LORD.

"You say, 'Do not prophesy against Israel,
        and do not preach against the house
            of Isaac.'

¹⁷ Therefore thus says the LORD:

"'Your wife shall be a prostitute in the city,
        and your sons and your daughters shall
            fall by the sword,
        and your land shall be divided up with a
            measuring line;
    you yourself shall die in an unclean land,
        and Israel shall surely go into exile away
            from its land.'"

1. Why does Amaziah want Amos to go back home to Judah?

2. Why did Amos come to Israel in the first place?

3. Does Amos stop preaching? Does he change his message at all? What does he say will happen to Amaziah and Amaziah's people?

PONDER With regard to his conduct, how does Amos compare to the apostles in Acts 5:27-32?[47]

PRAYER IDEAS Praise God that he is worthy of the loyalty of his people, even when that loyalty comes under fire. Ask him to help you to be loyal to him—even if you are persecuted for it.

READING 38   AMOS 8:1-14

This is what the Lord GOD showed me: behold, a basket of summer fruit. ² And he said, "Amos, what do you see?" And I said, "A basket of summer fruit." Then the LORD said to me,

"The end has come upon my people Israel;
    I will never again pass by them.
³ The songs of the temple shall become
        wailings in that day,"
                    declares the Lord GOD.

"So many dead bodies!"
"They are thrown everywhere!"
"Silence!"

⁴ Hear this, you who trample on the needy
        and bring the poor of the land to an end,
⁵ saying, "When will the new moon be over,
        that we may sell grain?
And the Sabbath,
        that we may offer wheat for sale,

---

47. And when they had brought them, they set them before the council. And the high priest questioned them, ²⁸ saying, "We strictly charged you not to teach in this name, yet here you have filled Jerusalem with your teaching, and you intend to bring this man's blood upon us." ²⁹ But Peter and the apostles answered, "We must obey God rather than men. ³⁰ The God of our fathers raised Jesus, whom you killed by hanging him on a tree. ³¹ God exalted him at his right hand as Leader and Savior, to give repentance to Israel and forgiveness of sins. ³² And we are witnesses to these things, and so is the Holy Spirit, whom God has given to those who obey him."

that we may make the ephah small and the
        shekel great
    and deal deceitfully with false balances,
⁶ that we may buy the poor for silver
    and the needy for a pair of sandals
    and sell the chaff of the wheat?"

⁷ The LORD has sworn by the pride of Jacob:
"Surely I will never forget any of their
        deeds.
⁸ Shall not the land tremble on this
        account,
    and everyone mourn who dwells in it,
and all of it rise like the Nile,
    and be tossed about and sink again, like
        the Nile of Egypt?"

⁹ "And on that day," declares the Lord GOD,
    "I will make the sun go down at noon
    and darken the earth in broad daylight.
¹⁰ I will turn your feasts into mourning
    and all your songs into lamentation;
I will bring sackcloth on every waist
    and baldness on every head;
I will make it like the mourning for an only
        son
    and the end of it like a bitter day.

¹¹ "Behold, the days are coming," declares
        the Lord GOD,
    "when I will send a famine on the
        land—
not a famine of bread, nor a thirst for
        water,
    but of hearing the words of the LORD.
¹² They shall wander from sea to sea,
    and from north to east;
they shall run to and fro, to seek the word
        of the LORD,
    but they shall not find it.

¹³ "In that day the lovely virgins and the
        young men
    shall faint for thirst.
¹⁴ Those who swear by the Guilt of Samaria,
    and say, 'As your god lives, O Dan,'
and, 'As the Way of Beersheba lives,'
    they shall fall, and never rise again."

*1. What is the significance of the silence at
    the end of verse 3?*

2. How has Israel sinned in this passage?

*3. What unusual punishment does God
    promise in verses 11-12?*

PONDER Israel asked that God's word
be taken away (remember Amaziah from
Reading 37). God in his righteous judgement
gives them exactly what they want. Read
Matthew 4:4.[48] Why is God's judgement
disastrous for Israel?

PRAYER IDEAS Thank God for giving you
true life through his word. Ask him to help
you to treasure his word instead of rejecting
it the way the Israelites did.

---

48. But he answered, "It is written,

"'Man shall not live by bread alone,
    but by every word that comes from the mouth of God.'"

I saw the LORD standing beside the altar, and he said:

"Strike the capitals until the thresholds
    shake,
    and shatter them on the heads of all
      the people;
and those who are left of them I will kill
    with the sword;
    not one of them shall flee away;
    not one of them shall escape.

2 "If they dig into Sheol,
    from there shall my hand take them;
if they climb up to heaven,
    from there I will bring them down.
3 If they hide themselves on the top of
      Carmel,
    from there I will search them out and
      take them;
and if they hide from my sight at the
      bottom of the sea,
    there I will command the serpent, and it
      shall bite them.
4 And if they go into captivity before their
      enemies,
    there I will command the sword, and it
      shall kill them;
and I will fix my eyes upon them
    for evil and not for good."

5 The Lord GOD of hosts,
he who touches the earth and it melts,
    and all who dwell in it mourn,
and all of it rises like the Nile,
    and sinks again, like the Nile of Egypt;
6 who builds his upper chambers in the
      heavens
    and founds his vault upon the earth;
who calls for the waters of the sea
    and pours them out upon the surface of
      the earth—
the LORD is his name.

7 "Are you not like the Cushites to me,
    O people of Israel?" declares the LORD.
"Did I not bring up Israel from the land of
      Egypt,
    and the Philistines from Caphtor and
      the Syrians from Kir?
8 Behold, the eyes of the Lord GOD are upon
      the sinful kingdom,
    and I will destroy it from the surface of
      the ground,
except that I will not utterly destroy the
      house of Jacob,"
                        declares the LORD.

9 "For behold, I will command,
    and shake the house of Israel among all
      the nations
as one shakes with a sieve,
    but no pebble shall fall to the earth.
10 All the sinners of my people shall die by
      the sword,
    who say, 'Disaster shall not overtake or
      meet us.'"

*1. What does it mean for Israel that God's
"eyes" are upon them (vv. 4, 8)?*

*2. What great promise does the word
"except" introduce in verse 8?*

*3. In verses 9-10, who will be killed and who
will be spared?*

PONDER Read Romans 3:23-26.[49] Who will be saved?

PRAYER IDEAS Praise God for being able to save sinners while remaining just. Thank him for making this possible through Jesus. Thank him for making this possible for you.

POINTER God in his wisdom and justice recognizes that, even though Israel is a "sinful kingdom" (v. 8), not all Israelites are "sinners" (v. 10). Of course, there is no such thing as a sinless Israelite. But God distinguishes between those who have rejected him ("sinners") and those who keep trusting him.

READING 40   AMOS 9:11-15

11 "In that day I will raise up
    the booth of David that is fallen
and repair its breaches,
    and raise up its ruins
    and rebuild it as in the days of old,
12 that they may possess the remnant of
        Edom
    and all the nations who are called by
        my name,"
    declares the LORD who does this.

13 "Behold, the days are coming," declares
        the LORD,
    "when the plowman shall overtake the
        reaper
    and the treader of grapes him who sows
        the seed;
the mountains shall drip sweet wine,
    and all the hills shall flow with it.
14 I will restore the fortunes of my people
        Israel,
    and they shall rebuild the ruined cities
        and inhabit them;
they shall plant vineyards and drink their
        wine,

and they shall make gardens and eat
        their fruit.
15 I will plant them on their land,
    and they shall never again be uprooted
    out of the land that I have given them,"
        says the LORD your God.

1. What will God do to the fallen "booth of David" (v. 11)?

2. Read the footnote to verse 12.[50] It is probably a better translation of the verse. What does this verse look forward to?

---

49. ... for all have sinned and fall short of the glory of God, 24 and are justified by his grace as a gift, through the redemption that is in Christ Jesus, 25 whom God put forward as a propitiation by his blood, to be received by faith. This was to show God's righteousness, because in his divine forbearance he had passed over former sins. 26 It was to show his righteousness at the present time, so that he might be just and the justifier of the one who has faith in Jesus.

50. Hebrew; Septuagint *that the remnant of mankind and all the nations who are called by my name may seek the Lord.* Compare Acts 15:17:

"'... that the remnant of mankind may seek the Lord,
    and all the Gentiles who are called by my name,
        says the Lord, who makes these things known ...'"

3. Read 5:11.[51] *Why do you think 9:14 is now saying something different?*

PRAYER IDEAS Thank God that the promises he made through Amos have come true in your experience, for you are now part of a family made up of both Jews and Gentiles. Praise him for including you in the shelter of his mercy.

PONDER In 722 BC, Israel was exiled in fulfilment of Amos's prophecy (e.g. 6:14).[52] So when were these promises in 9:11-15 fulfilled? Read Acts 15:4-18 in the Appendix (pp. 71-72). How were Amos's words being fulfilled at the time of the apostles?

POINTER v. 11: The "booth of David" probably refers to the city of Jerusalem or, perhaps more broadly, the kingdom of David. Given the permanence suggested by verse 15, it may even point forward in part to a heavenly reality still to come.

---

51. Therefore because you trample on the poor
and you exact taxes of grain from him,
you have built houses of hewn stone,
but you shall not dwell in them;
you have planted pleasant vineyards,
but you shall not drink their wine.

52. "For behold, I will raise up against you a nation,
O house of Israel," declares the Lord, the God of hosts;
"and they shall oppress you from Lebo-hamath
to the Brook of the Arabah."

2 CORINTHIANS

INTRODUCTION

2 Corinthians seems to have been written very soon after 1 Corinthians. However, much took place in the interim period. Paul visited Corinth initially for 18 months (Acts 18:11).[53] Then he wrote them two letters. The first was not preserved (but it is referred to in 1 Corinthians 5:9)[54] and the second was the book of 1 Corinthians. Paul then had another "painful visit" to them, during which he was severely shunned (2 Cor 1:23-2:4).[55] Instead of planning a third visit, he sent the 'severe letter' (again, not preserved, but some think that this was the book of 1 Corinthians). He then waited anxiously from Titus to find out how that letter was received (2 Cor 2:9,[56] 13[57]). Would the Corinthians reject God's messenger?

When Paul receives the great news that God's Spirit is alive in the Corinthians (2 Cor 7:5-9),[58] he pens the book of 2 Corinthians. In chapters 1-7, he defends and re-establishes his apostolic authority; in chapters 8-9, he calls for a new start in the relief effort; and then in chapters 10-13, he shifts gears to attack those who wish to discredit him and those who would follow these people. This is all done in preparation for his third visit.

This defence of God's apostle is a timely reminder to us as we live in an age when many (including those within the church) stridently dismiss God's right to have a say on anything that seems out of vogue. On the one hand, Paul's passion to defend the truth, stemming from the meekness and gentleness of Christ, is something we would do well to adopt; on the other hand, Paul's boldness in calling for relief money and exposing God's enemies challenges us to stand firm in what we believe.

---

53. And he stayed a year and six months, teaching the word of God among them.
54. I wrote to you in my letter not to associate with sexually immoral people ...
55. But I call God to witness against me—it was to spare you that I refrained from coming again to Corinth. 24 Not that we lord it over your faith, but we work with you for your joy, for you stand firm in your faith.
  2:1 For I made up my mind not to make another painful visit to you. 2 For if I cause you pain, who is there to make me glad but the one whom I have pained? 3 And I wrote as I did, so that when I came I might not suffer pain from those who should have made me rejoice, for I felt sure of all of you, that my joy would be the joy of you all. 4 For I wrote to you out of much affliction and anguish of heart and with many tears, not to cause you pain but to let you know the abundant love that I have for you.

56. For this is why I wrote, that I might test you and know whether you are obedient in everything.
57. ... my spirit was not at rest because I did not find my brother Titus there. So I took leave of them and went on to Macedonia.
58. For even when we came into Macedonia, our bodies had no rest, but we were afflicted at every turn—fighting without and fear within. 6 But God, who comforts the downcast, comforted us by the coming of Titus, 7 and not only by his coming but also by the comfort with which he was comforted by you, as he told us of your longing, your mourning, your zeal for me, so that I rejoiced still more. 8 For even if I made you grieve with my letter, I do not regret it—though I did regret it, for I see that that letter grieved you, though only for a while. 9 As it is, I rejoice, not because you were grieved, but because you were grieved into repenting. For you felt a godly grief, so that you suffered no loss through us.

You might like to use this prayer (or your own variation on it) before each of the next 20 studies:

Dear Heavenly Father,
Thank you for the Apostle Paul and his defence of the truth. Please keep me from departing from the truth, and help me to defend the truth carefully and boldly so that your kingdom will continue to grow throughout this lost world.
Amen.

READING 41   2 CORINTHIANS 1:1-11

Paul, an apostle of Christ Jesus by the will of God, and Timothy our brother,

To the church of God that is at Corinth, with all the saints who are in the whole of Achaia:

2 Grace to you and peace from God our Father and the Lord Jesus Christ.

3 Blessed be the God and Father of our Lord Jesus Christ, the Father of mercies and God of all comfort, 4 who comforts us in all our affliction, so that we may be able to comfort those who are in any affliction, with the comfort with which we ourselves are comforted by God. 5 For as we share abundantly in Christ's sufferings, so through Christ we share abundantly in comfort too. 6 If we are afflicted, it is for your comfort and salvation; and if we are comforted, it is for your comfort, which you experience when you patiently endure the same sufferings that we suffer. 7 Our hope for you is unshaken, for we know that as you share in our sufferings, you will also share in our comfort.

8 For we do not want you to be ignorant, brothers, of the affliction we experienced in Asia. For we were so utterly burdened beyond our strength that we despaired of life itself.

9 Indeed, we felt that we had received the sentence of death. But that was to make us rely not on ourselves but on God who raises the dead. 10 He delivered us from such a deadly peril, and he will deliver us. On him we have set our hope that he will deliver us again. 11 You also must help us by prayer, so that many will give thanks on our behalf for the blessing granted us through the prayers of many.

1. Verse 1 says that Paul and Timothy have both written this letter, but verse 15[59] is written in the first person singular (i.e. 'I'). Do you think the verses in first person plural (i.e. 'we') refer to Paul alone, or to both Paul and Timothy?

2. How does the God of all comfort actually comfort (cf. 2:14,[60] 7:4-7[61])?

---

59. Because I was sure of this, I wanted to come to you first, so that you might have a second experience of grace.
60. But thanks be to God, who in Christ always leads us in triumphal procession, and through us spreads the fragrance of the knowledge of him everywhere.
61. I am acting with great boldness toward you; I have great pride in you; I am filled with comfort. In all our affliction, I am overflowing with joy.

5 For even when we came into Macedonia, our bodies had no rest, but we were afflicted at every turn—fighting without and fear within. 6 But God, who comforts the downcast, comforted us by the coming of Titus, 7 and not only by his coming but also by the comfort with which he was comforted by you, as he told us of your longing, your mourning, your zeal for me, so that I rejoiced still more.

PONDER When a Christian friend is in need of comfort, how does this passage help you to comfort them?

PRAYER IDEAS Pray for those you know in need: ask God to help them. Thank him for being the Father of mercies and the God of all comfort.

POINTER It seems like most of Paul's plural references (e.g. 'we', 'us', 'our') refer to him alone. In the rest of the letter, 'we' will often refer just to 'Paul'. As you read, it's worth asking why Paul alternates between first person singular and first person plural.

READING 42   2 CORINTHIANS 1:12-2:4

For our boast is this, the testimony of our conscience, that we behaved in the world with simplicity and godly sincerity, not by earthly wisdom but by the grace of God, and supremely so toward you. [13] For we are not writing to you anything other than what you read and acknowledge and I hope you will fully acknowledge— [14] just as you did partially acknowledge us—that on the day of our Lord Jesus you will boast of us as we will boast of you.

[15] Because I was sure of this, I wanted to come to you first, so that you might have a second experience of grace. [16] I wanted to visit you on my way to Macedonia, and to come back to you from Macedonia and have you send me on my way to Judea. [17] Was I vacillating when I wanted to do this? Do I make my plans according to the flesh, ready to say "Yes, yes" and "No, no" at the same time? [18] As surely as God is faithful, our word to you has not been Yes and No. [19] For the Son of God, Jesus Christ, whom we proclaimed among you, Silvanus and Timothy and I, was not Yes and No, but in him it is always Yes. [20] For all the promises of God find their Yes in him. That is why it is through him that we utter our Amen to God for his glory. [21] And it is God who establishes us with you in Christ, and has anointed us, [22] and who has also put his seal on us and given us his Spirit in our hearts as a guarantee.

[23] But I call God to witness against me—it was to spare you that I refrained from coming again to Corinth. [24] Not that we lord it over your faith, but we work with you for your joy, for you stand firm in your faith.

2:1 For I made up my mind not to make another painful visit to you. [2] For if I cause you pain, who is there to make me glad but the one whom I have pained? [3] And I wrote as I did, so that when I came I might not suffer pain from those who should have made me rejoice, for I felt sure of all of you, that my joy would be the joy of you all. [4] For I wrote to you out of much affliction and anguish of heart and with many tears, not to cause you pain but to let you know the abundant love that I have for you.

1. What are Paul's motives for behaving the way he does (1:12-17)?

2. What are his motives based on (1:18-22)?

3. Why did he write the letter of 1 Corinthians (see the introduction on p. 49) rather than make his third visit as planned (1:23-2:4)?

PONDER What motivates you? What should change in your motivations? What concrete steps will you take in order to change?

PRAYER IDEAS Ask God to help you to be consistent in your motives toward others, no matter what the circumstances.

Now if anyone has caused pain, he has caused it not to me, but in some measure—not to put it too severely—to all of you. [6] For such a one, this punishment by the majority is enough, [7] so you should rather turn to forgive and comfort him, or he may be overwhelmed by excessive sorrow. [8] So I beg you to reaffirm your love for him. [9] For this is why I wrote, that I might test you and know whether you are obedient in everything. [10] Anyone whom you forgive, I also forgive. Indeed, what I have forgiven, if I have forgiven anything, has been for your sake in the presence of Christ, [11] so that we would not be outwitted by Satan; for we are not ignorant of his designs.

[12] When I came to Troas to preach the gospel of Christ, even though a door was opened for me in the Lord, [13] my spirit was not at rest because I did not find my brother Titus there. So I took leave of them and went on to Macedonia.

1. Read the pointer. What do you learn about applying discipline to fellow believers?

2. If Paul is so keen to restore a repentant believer, what do you think is Satan's plan?

3. What was the extent of Paul's concern to hear from Titus how his 'severe letter' was received (see pointer)?

PONDER Do you know any wayward Christians? Have you tried to restore them?

PRAYER IDEAS Ask God to keep his children from wandering. Ask him to give you boldness to bring his warning and comfort to those who do.

POINTER v. 6: Traditionally, this person has been identified as the incestuous man of 1 Corinthians 5:1-5.[62] However, an equally valid reading is that this man was the ringleader of the group who had thwarted Paul's authority on his second "painful visit" (2 Cor 2:1;[63] cf. 7:12[64]).

---

62. It is actually reported that there is sexual immorality among you, and of a kind that is not tolerated even among pagans, for a man has his father's wife. [2] And you are arrogant! Ought you not rather to mourn? Let him who has done this be removed from among you.

[3] For though absent in body, I am present in spirit; and as if present, I have already pronounced judgment on the one who did such a thing. [4] When you are assembled in the name of the Lord Jesus and my spirit is present, with the power of our Lord Jesus, [5] you are to deliver this man to Satan for the destruction of the flesh, so that his spirit may be saved in the day of the Lord.

63. For I made up my mind not to make another painful visit to you.

64. So although I wrote to you, it was not for the sake of the one who did the wrong, nor for the sake of the one who suffered the wrong, but in order that your earnestness for us might be revealed to you in the sight of God.

But thanks be to God, who in Christ always leads us in triumphal procession, and through us spreads the fragrance of the knowledge of him everywhere. ¹⁵ For we are the aroma of Christ to God among those who are being saved and among those who are perishing, ¹⁶ to one a fragrance from death to death, to the other a fragrance from life to life. Who is sufficient for these things? ¹⁷ For we are not, like so many, peddlers of God's word, but as men of sincerity, as commissioned by God, in the sight of God we speak in Christ.

3:1 Are we beginning to commend ourselves again? Or do we need, as some do, letters of recommendation to you, or from you? ² You yourselves are our letter of recommendation, written on our hearts, to be known and read by all. ³ And you show that you are a letter from Christ delivered by us, written not with ink but with the Spirit of the living God, not on tablets of stone but on tablets of human hearts.

⁴ Such is the confidence that we have through Christ toward God. ⁵ Not that we are sufficient in ourselves to claim anything as coming from us, but our sufficiency is from God, ⁶ who has made us competent to be ministers of a new covenant, not of the letter but of the Spirit. For the letter kills, but the Spirit gives life.

1. Having defended his past actions, how does Paul view his ministry (2:14-17)?

2. How do Paul's "letters of recommendation" commend him (3:1-3)?

3. What makes Paul "sufficient" in his ministry (3:4-6)?

PONDER　How does God equip his people for his mission?

PRAYER IDEAS　Thank God for the confidence you can have "through Christ toward God" (3:4).

Now if the ministry of death, carved in letters on stone, came with such glory that the Israelites could not gaze at Moses' face because of its glory, which was being brought to an end, ⁸ will not the ministry of the Spirit have even more glory? ⁹ For if there was glory in the ministry of condemnation, the ministry of righteousness must far exceed it in glory. ¹⁰ Indeed, in this case, what once had glory has come to have no glory at all, because of the glory that surpasses it. ¹¹ For if what was being brought to an end came with glory, much more will what is permanent have glory.

¹² Since we have such a hope, we are very bold, ¹³ not like Moses, who would put a veil over his face so that the Israelites might not gaze at the outcome of what was being brought to an end. ¹⁴ But their minds were hardened. For to this day, when they read the old covenant, that same veil remains unlifted, because only through Christ is it taken away. ¹⁵ Yes, to this day whenever Moses is read a veil lies over their hearts. ¹⁶ But when one

LUKE 1-6

AMOS

2 CORINTHIANS

turns to the Lord, the veil is removed. [17] Now the Lord is the Spirit, and where the Spirit of the Lord is, there is freedom. [18] And we all, with unveiled face, beholding the glory of the Lord, are being transformed into the same image from one degree of glory to another. For this comes from the Lord who is the Spirit.

1. How glorious was the old covenant's ministry of "death" and "condemnation" (cf. Exod 34:29-35)? [65]

2. If the new covenant's ministry of "the Spirit" and "righteousness" will never end, what is the place of the old covenant's ministry?

3. Moses wanted to veil the 'glory' (i.e. the magnificence of God) of the old covenant to stop people being fixated by it (v. 13). What was the problem in Paul's day?

4. How is the veil removed and what is the outcome of its removal?

PONDER Who is veiled amongst your colleagues, friends and family? What opportunities do you see for the veil to be removed from them?

PRAYER IDEAS Thank God for the incredible and glorious ministry that Christ has provided.

READING 46   2 CORINTHIANS 4:1-6

Therefore, having this ministry by the mercy of God, we do not lose heart. [2] But we have renounced disgraceful, underhanded ways. We refuse to practice cunning or to tamper with God's word, but by the open statement of the truth we would commend ourselves to everyone's conscience in the sight of God. [3] And even if our gospel is veiled, it is veiled only to those who are perishing. [4] In their case the god of this world has blinded the minds of the unbelievers, to keep them from seeing the light of the gospel of the glory of Christ, who is the image of God. [5] For what we proclaim is not ourselves, but Jesus Christ as Lord, with ourselves as your servants for Jesus' sake. [6] For God, who said, "Let light shine out of darkness," has shone in our hearts to give the

---

65. When Moses came down from Mount Sinai, with the two tablets of the testimony in his hand as he came down from the mountain, Moses did not know that the skin of his face shone because he had been talking with God. [30] Aaron and all the people of Israel saw Moses, and behold, the skin of his face shone, and they were afraid to come near him. [31] But Moses called to them, and Aaron and all the leaders of the congregation returned to him, and Moses talked with them. [32] Afterward all the people of Israel came near, and he commanded them all that the Lord had spoken with him in Mount Sinai. [33] And when Moses had finished speaking with them, he put a veil over his face.
[34] Whenever Moses went in before the Lord to speak with him, he would remove the veil, until he came out. And when he came out and told the people of Israel what he was commanded, [35] the people of Israel would see the face of Moses, that the skin of Moses' face was shining. And Moses would put the veil over his face again, until he went in to speak with him.

light of the knowledge of the glory of God in the face of Jesus Christ.

1. What is Paul's ministry method?

2. How does Paul answer those who would say his ministry has failed?

3. Paul refers to the first day of creation in verse 6. What does he compare it to?

What is he suggesting by making this comparison (cf. 5:17)? [66]

PONDER Paul says he conducted his ministry "by the open statement of the truth" (v. 2). What are the implications for the way ministry should be conducted if you take Paul as a model?

PRAYER IDEAS Ask God to remove all the disgraceful and underhanded ways of tampering with his word from all Christian ministry, including your own. Ask him to make "the open statement of the truth" central to both your Christian witness and that of others.

But we have this treasure in jars of clay, to show that the surpassing power belongs to God and not to us. 8 We are afflicted in every way, but not crushed; perplexed, but not driven to despair; 9 persecuted, but not forsaken; struck down, but not destroyed; 10 always carrying in the body the death of Jesus, so that the life of Jesus may also be manifested in our bodies. 11 For we who live are always being given over to death for Jesus' sake, so that the life of Jesus also may be manifested in our mortal flesh. 12 So death is at work in us, but life in you.

13 Since we have the same spirit of faith according to what has been written, "I believed, and so I spoke," we also believe, and so we also speak, 14 knowing that he who raised the Lord Jesus will raise us also with Jesus and bring us with you into his presence. 15 For it is all for your sake, so that as grace extends to more and more people it may increase thanksgiving, to the glory of God.

1. What is the "treasure" and what are the "jars of clay" (v. 7)?

2. Why do you think God has made it this way?

PONDER How does this imagery explain the Christian experience? What is the place in the Christian life of expectations of health, wealth and success?

PRAYER IDEAS Ask God to ensure that all the ministries in your church will rely on God's surpassing power and not on their own attractiveness.

---

66. Therefore, if anyone is in Christ, he is a new creation. The old has passed away; behold, the new has come.

LUKE 1-6

AMOS

2 CORINTHIANS

So we do not lose heart. Though our outer self is wasting away, our inner self is being renewed day by day. [17] For this light momentary affliction is preparing for us an eternal weight of glory beyond all comparison, [18] as we look not to the things that are seen but to the things that are unseen. For the things that are seen are transient, but the things that are unseen are eternal.

5:1 For we know that if the tent that is our earthly home is destroyed, we have a building from God, a house not made with hands, eternal in the heavens. [2] For in this tent we groan, longing to put on our heavenly dwelling, [3] if indeed by putting it on we may not be found naked. [4] For while we are still in this tent, we groan, being burdened—not that we would be unclothed, but that we would be further clothed, so that what is mortal may be swallowed up by life. [5] He who has prepared us for this very thing is God, who has given us the Spirit as a guarantee.

[6] So we are always of good courage. We know that while we are at home in the body we are away from the Lord, [7] for we walk by faith, not by sight. [8] Yes, we are of good courage, and we would rather be away from the body and at home with the Lord. [9] So whether we are at home or away, we make it our aim to please him. [10] For we must all appear before the judgment seat of Christ, so that each one may receive what is due for what he has done in the body, whether good or evil.

1. What do you think would have been making Paul "lose heart" (v. 16)?

2. How does Paul not "lose heart"?

3. Why does Paul make it his aim to please God?

PONDER How do you cope with setbacks which make you lose heart? How fundamental is the life to come to your everyday thinking?

PRAYER IDEAS Ask God to aid those you know who are afflicted. Ask him to give you a fuller perspective to prepare you for suffering when it comes.

Therefore, knowing the fear of the Lord, we persuade others. But what we are is known to God, and I hope it is known also to your conscience. [12] We are not commending ourselves to you again but giving you cause to boast about us, so that you may be able to answer those who boast about outward appearance and not about what is in the heart. [13] For if we are beside ourselves, it is for God; if we are in our right mind, it is for you. [14] For the love of Christ controls us, because we have concluded this: that one has died for all, therefore all have died; [15] and he died for all, that those who live might no longer live for themselves but for him who for their sake died and was raised.

[16] From now on, therefore, we regard no one according to the flesh. Even though we

once regarded Christ according to the flesh, we regard him thus no longer. [17] Therefore, if anyone is in Christ, he is a new creation. The old has passed away; behold, the new has come. [18] All this is from God, who through Christ reconciled us to himself and gave us the ministry of reconciliation; [19] that is, in Christ God was reconciling the world to himself, not counting their trespasses against them, and entrusting to us the message of reconciliation. [20] Therefore, we are ambassadors for Christ, God making his appeal through us. We implore you on behalf of Christ, be reconciled to God. [21] For our sake he made him to be sin who knew no sin, so that in him we might become the righteousness of God.

6:1 Working together with him, then, we appeal to you not to receive the grace of God in vain. [2] For he says,

"In a favorable time I listened to you,
        and in a day of salvation I have helped you."

Behold, now is the favorable time; behold, now is the day of salvation.

1. What motivates Paul?

2. In this "ministry of reconciliation" (5:18), what roles do God, Christ and human ambassadors play?

3. What does Paul say about "now"—that is, the times in which we live (5:16, 6:2)?

PONDER What part do you play in this "ministry of reconciliation"?

PRAYER IDEAS Ask God to ensure that Christ's love controls you continually so that you no longer live for yourself but for "him who for [your] sake died and was raised" (5:15).

READING 50   2 CORINTHIANS 6:3-10

We put no obstacle in anyone's way, so that no fault may be found with our ministry, [4] but as servants of God we commend ourselves in every way: by great endurance, in afflictions, hardships, calamities, [5] beatings, imprisonments, riots, labors, sleepless nights, hunger; [6] by purity, knowledge, patience, kindness, the Holy Spirit, genuine love; [7] by truthful speech, and the power of God; with the weapons of righteousness for the right hand and for the left; [8] through honor and dishonor, through slander and praise. We are treated as impostors, and yet are true; [9] as unknown, and yet well known; as dying, and behold, we live; as punished, and yet not killed; [10] as sorrowful, yet always rejoicing; as poor, yet making many rich; as having nothing, yet possessing everything.

1. Write a list of everything that Paul says to commend himself.

LUKE 1-6

AMOS

2 CORINTHIANS

2. Given this list, what is surprising about what Paul is saying in this passage?

PONDER How can you prepare yourself better to stand firm in the truth?

PRAYER IDEAS Ask God to strengthen the resolve of Christians throughout the world so they will stand firm in the face of horrific and subtle opposition.

READING 51   2 CORINTHIANS 6:11-7:4 ■

We have spoken freely to you, Corinthians; our heart is wide open. ¹² You are not restricted by us, but you are restricted in your own affections. ¹³ In return (I speak as to children) widen your hearts also.

¹⁴ Do not be unequally yoked with unbelievers. For what partnership has righteousness with lawlessness? Or what fellowship has light with darkness? ¹⁵ What accord has Christ with Belial? Or what portion does a believer share with an unbeliever? ¹⁶ What agreement has the temple of God with idols? For we are the temple of the living God; as God said,

"I will make my dwelling among them and
        walk among them,
    and I will be their God,
    and they shall be my people.
¹⁷ Therefore go out from their midst,
    and be separate from them, says the
        Lord,
and touch no unclean thing;
    then I will welcome you,
¹⁸ and I will be a father to you,
    and you shall be sons and daughters
        to me,
says the Lord Almighty."

7:1 Since we have these promises, beloved, let us cleanse ourselves from every defilement of body and spirit, bringing holiness to completion in the fear of God.

² Make room in your hearts for us. We have wronged no one, we have corrupted no one,

we have taken advantage of no one. ³ I do not say this to condemn you, for I said before that you are in our hearts, to die together and to live together. ⁴ I am acting with great boldness toward you; I have great pride in you; I am filled with comfort. In all our affliction, I am overflowing with joy.

1. In 6:11-13 and 7:2-4 what do you learn about the intensity of Paul's ministry and the situation in Corinth?

2. What do these 'bookend' verses suggest about the subject matter of the verses in between (6:14-7:1)?

3. How severe does Paul consider their rejection of him?

4. Why do you think Paul makes an extended defence of himself in chapters 1-6?

PONDER What is Paul's place in salvation history? What should your attitude be towards him?

PRAYER IDEAS Ask God to open your heart to Paul and to help you to separate yourself from anything that prevents you from hearing his words.

READING 52   2 CORINTHIANS 7:5-16

For even when we came into Macedonia, our bodies had no rest, but we were afflicted at every turn—fighting without and fear within. [6] But God, who comforts the downcast, comforted us by the coming of Titus, [7] and not only by his coming but also by the comfort with which he was comforted by you, as he told us of your longing, your mourning, your zeal for me, so that I rejoiced still more. [8] For even if I made you grieve with my letter, I do not regret it—though I did regret it, for I see that that letter grieved you, though only for a while. [9] As it is, I rejoice, not because you were grieved, but because you were grieved into repenting. For you felt a godly grief, so that you suffered no loss through us.

[10] For godly grief produces a repentance that leads to salvation without regret, whereas worldly grief produces death. [11] For see what earnestness this godly grief has produced in you, but also what eagerness to clear yourselves, what indignation, what fear, what longing, what zeal, what punishment! At every point you have proved yourselves innocent in the matter. [12] So although I wrote to you, it was not for the sake of the one who did the wrong, nor for the sake of the one who suffered the wrong, but in order that your earnestness for us might be revealed to you in the sight of God. [13] Therefore we are comforted.

And besides our own comfort, we rejoiced still more at the joy of Titus, because his spirit has been refreshed by you all. [14] For whatever boasts I made to him about you, I was not put to shame. But just as everything we said to you was true, so also our boasting before Titus has proved true. [15] And his affection for you is even greater, as he remembers the obedience of you all, how you received him with fear and trembling. [16] I rejoice, because I have perfect confidence in you.

1. Paul says he is enduring affliction, yet he is filled with comfort and overflowing with joy. Why?

2. Why does Paul both regret and not regret writing the Corinthians a letter which made them 'grieve' (vv. 8-9)?

3. How effective was that letter? What did the Corinthians do as a result? What role did Titus play?

PONDER What is the difference between "worldly grief" and "godly grief" (v. 10)? Is "godly grief" something you've felt?

PRAYER IDEAS Ask God to help you to desire the comfort of seeing other Christians standing firm in the Lord.

LUKE 1-6

AMOS

2 CORINTHIANS

We want you to know, brothers, about the grace of God that has been given among the churches of Macedonia, 2 for in a severe test of affliction, their abundance of joy and their extreme poverty have overflowed in a wealth of generosity on their part. 3 For they gave according to their means, as I can testify, and beyond their means, of their own accord, 4 begging us earnestly for the favor of taking part in the relief of the saints— 5 and this, not as we expected, but they gave themselves first to the Lord and then by the will of God to us. 6 Accordingly, we urged Titus that as he had started, so he should complete among you this act of grace. 7 But as you excel in everything—in faith, in speech, in knowledge, in all earnestness, and in our love for you— see that you excel in this act of grace also.

8 I say this not as a command, but to prove by the earnestness of others that your love also is genuine. 9 For you know the grace of our Lord Jesus Christ, that though he was rich, yet for your sake he became poor, so that you by his poverty might become rich. 10 And in this matter I give my judgment: this benefits you, who a year ago started not only to do this work but also to desire to do it. 11 So now finish doing it as well, so that your readiness in desiring it may be matched by your completing it out of what you have. 12 For if the readiness is there, it is acceptable according to what a person has, not according to what he does not have. 13 For I do not meanthat others should be eased and you burdened, but that as a matter of fairness 14 your abundance at the present time should supply their need, so that their abundance may supply your need, that there may be fairness. 15 As it is written, "Whoever gathered much had nothing left over, and whoever gathered little had no lack."

16 But thanks be to God, who put into the heart of Titus the same earnest care I have for you. 17 For he not only accepted our appeal, but being himself very earnest he is going to you of his own accord. 18 With him we are sending the brother who is famous among all the churches for his preaching of the gospel. 19 And not only that, but he has been appointed by the churches to travel with us as we carry out this act of grace that is being ministered by us, for the glory of the Lord himself and to show our good will. 20 We take this course so that no one should blame us about this generous gift that is being administered by us, 21 for we aim at what is honorable not only in the Lord's sight but also in the sight of man. 22 And with them we are sending our brother whom we have often tested and found earnest in many matters, but who is now more earnest than ever because of his great confidence in you. 23 As for Titus, he is my partner and fellow worker for your benefit. And as for our brothers, they are messengers of the churches, the glory of Christ. 24 So give proof before the churches of your love and of our boasting about you to these men.

9:1 Now it is superfluous for me to write to you about the ministry for the saints, 2 for I know your readiness, of which I boast about you to the people of Macedonia, saying that Achaia has been ready since last year. And your zeal has stirred up most of them. 3 But I am sending the brothers so that our boasting about you may not prove empty in this matter, so that you may be ready, as I said you would be. 4 Otherwise, if some Macedonians come with me and find that you are not ready, we would be humiliated—to say nothing of you—for being so confident. 5 So I thought it necessary to urge the brothers to go on ahead to you and arrange in advance for the gift you have promised, so that it may be ready as a willing gift, not as an exaction.

1. How was the Macedonians' generosity (8:1-7) a good motivation for the Corinthians to resume their collection for "the relief of the saints" (i.e. the poor Christians in Jerusalem; cf. 1 Cor 16:1-4)?[67]

2. What objections do you think Paul was anticipating when he wrote 8:8-15?

3. Who are the three men who are going to Corinth (8:16-9:5)? Why are they going? What does Paul say about them?

PONDER What measures does Paul take to ensure that he is blameless when it comes to the collection of the money?

PRAYER IDEAS Ask God to send relief to poor Christians around the world. Ask him to give you genuine concern for your fellow believers.

The point is this: whoever sows sparingly will also reap sparingly, and whoever sows bountifully will also reap bountifully. [7] Each one must give as he has decided in his heart, not reluctantly or under compulsion, for God loves a cheerful giver. [8] And God is able to make all grace abound to you, so that having all sufficiency in all things at all times, you may abound in every good work. [9] As it is written,

"He has distributed freely, he has given to the poor;
his righteousness endures forever."

[10] He who supplies seed to the sower and bread for food will supply and multiply your seed for sowing and increase the harvest of your righteousness. [11] You will be enriched in every way to be generous in every way, which through us will produce thanksgiving to God. [12] For the ministry of this service is not only supplying the needs of the saints but is also overflowing in many thanksgivings to God. [13] By their approval of this service, they will glorify God because of your submission flowing from your confession of the gospel of Christ, and the generosity of your contribution for them and for all others, [14] while they long for you and pray for you, because of the surpassing grace of God upon you. [15] Thanks be to God for his inexpressible gift!

1. What should motivate the Corinthians to be generous?

2. What does God love?

67. Now concerning the collection for the saints: as I directed the churches of Galatia, so you also are to do. [2] On the first day of every week, each of you is to put something aside and store it up, as he may prosper, so that there will be no collecting when I come. [3] And when I arrive, I will send those whom you accredit by letter to carry your gift to Jerusalem. [4] If it seems advisable that I should go also, they will accompany me.

LUKE 1-6

AMOS

2 CORINTHIANS

3. What is the outcome of their giving?

PONDER What motivates your giving? How are you investing in eternal things?

PRAYER IDEAS Thank God for the Christians you know who stand out in the way they operate because they utilize a very different investment strategy to the materialistic world.

READING 55   2 CORINTHIANS 10:1-18

I Paul, myself entreat you, by the meekness and gentleness of Christ—I who am humble when face to face with you, but bold toward you when I am away!— 2 I beg of you that when I am present I may not have to show boldness with such confidence as I count on showing against some who suspect us of walking according to the flesh. 3 For though we walk in the flesh, we are not waging war according to the flesh. 4 For the weapons of our warfare are not of the flesh but have divine power to destroy strongholds. 5 We destroy arguments and every lofty opinion raised against the knowledge of God, and take every thought captive to obey Christ, 6 being ready to punish every disobedience, when your obedience is complete.

7 Look at what is before your eyes. If anyone is confident that he is Christ's, let him remind himself that just as he is Christ's, so also are we. 8 For even if I boast a little too much of our authority, which the Lord gave for building you up and not for destroying you, I will not be ashamed. 9 I do not want to appear to be frightening you with my letters. 10 For they say, "His letters are weighty and strong, but his bodily presence is weak, and his speech of no account." 11 Let such a person understand that what we say by letter when absent, we do when present. 12 Not that we dare to classify or compare ourselves with some of those who are commending themselves. But when they measure themselves by one another and compare themselves with one another, they are without understanding.

13 But we will not boast beyond limits, but will boast only with regard to the area of influence God assigned to us, to reach even to you. 14 For we are not overextending ourselves, as though we did not reach you. For we were the first to come all the way to you with the gospel of Christ. 15 We do not boast beyond limit in the labors of others. But our hope is that as your faith increases, our area of influence among you may be greatly enlarged, 16 so that we may preach the gospel in lands beyond you, without boasting of work already done in another's area of influence. 17 "Let the one who boasts, boast in the Lord." 18 For it is not the one who commends himself who is approved, but the one whom the Lord commends.

1. What type of weapons does Paul use to wage war for God (vv. 1-6)? How effective are they?

2. What does Paul say about his authority and where it comes from (vv. 7-12)? What makes it incomparable?

3. What are Paul's future missionary plans (vv. 13-16)?

4. How does God commend Paul (v. 18)?

PONDER How do you regard Paul's authority? Is it easy for you to submit to his teaching?

PRAYER IDEAS Ask God to help Christian leaders to exercise the authority he has given them properly and to seek God's commendation above all.

READING 56   2 CORINTHIANS 11:1-21a

I wish you would bear with me in a little foolishness. Do bear with me! [2] For I feel a divine jealousy for you, since I betrothed you to one husband, to present you as a pure virgin to Christ. [3] But I am afraid that as the serpent deceived Eve by his cunning, your thoughts will be led astray from a sincere and pure devotion to Christ. [4] For if someone comes and proclaims another Jesus than the one we proclaimed, or if you receive a different spirit from the one you received, or if you accept a different gospel from the one you accepted, you put up with it readily enough. [5] Indeed, I consider that I am not in the least inferior to these super-apostles. [6] Even if I am unskilled in speaking, I am not so in knowledge; indeed, in every way we have made this plain to you in all things.

[7] Or did I commit a sin in humbling myself so that you might be exalted, because I preached God's gospel to you free of charge? [8] I robbed other churches by accepting support from them in order to serve you. [9] And when I was with you and was in need, I did not burden anyone, for the brothers who came from Macedonia supplied my need. So I refrained and will refrain from burdening you in any way. [10] As the truth of Christ is in me, this boasting of mine will not be silenced in the regions of Achaia. [11] And why? Because I do not love you? God knows I do!

[12] And what I do I will continue to do, in order to undermine the claim of those who would like to claim that in their boasted

mission they work on the same terms as we do. [13] For such men are false apostles, deceitful workmen, disguising themselves as apostles of Christ. [14] And no wonder, for even Satan disguises himself as an angel of light. [15] So it is no surprise if his servants, also, disguise themselves as servants of righteousness. Their end will correspond to their deeds.

[16] I repeat, let no one think me foolish. But even if you do, accept me as a fool, so that I too may boast a little. [17] What I am saying with this boastful confidence, I say not with the Lord's authority but as a fool. [18] Since many boast according to the flesh, I too will boast. [19] For you gladly bear with fools, being wise yourselves! [20] For you bear it if someone makes slaves of you, or devours you, or takes advantage of you, or puts on airs, or strikes you in the face. [21] To my shame, I must say, we were too weak for that!

1. Why was Paul so 'divinely jealous' for the Corinthians (vv. 1-3)?

2. Where were the Corinthians going wrong?

3. How does Paul demonstrate his integrity?

LUKE 1-6

AMOS

2 CORINTHIANS

PONDER How can you guard against Satan's ways?

PRAYER IDEAS Ask God to guard Christian leaders against Satan's ways.

READING 57   2 CORINTHIANS 11:21b-33

But whatever anyone else dares to boast of—I am speaking as a fool—I also dare to boast of that. 22 Are they Hebrews? So am I. Are they Israelites? So am I. Are they offspring of Abraham? So am I. 23 Are they servants of Christ? I am a better one—I am talking like a madman—with far greater labors, far more imprisonments, with countless beatings, and often near death. 24 Five times I received at the hands of the Jews the forty lashes less one. 25 Three times I was beaten with rods. Once I was stoned. Three times I was shipwrecked; a night and a day I was adrift at sea; 26 on frequent journeys, in danger from rivers, danger from robbers, danger from my own people, danger from Gentiles, danger in the city, danger in the wilderness, danger at sea, danger from false brothers; 27 in toil and hardship, through many a sleepless night, in hunger and thirst, often without food, in cold and exposure. 28 And, apart from other things, there is the daily pressure on me of my anxiety for all the churches. 29 Who is weak, and I am not weak? Who is made to fall, and I am not indignant?

30 If I must boast, I will boast of the things that show my weakness. 31 The God and Father of the Lord Jesus, he who is blessed forever, knows that I am not lying. 32 At Damascus, the governor under King Aretas

was guarding the city of Damascus in order to seize me, 33 but I was let down in a basket through a window in the wall and escaped his hands.

1. Paul loathed promoting himself, yet here he was forced to defend himself. How qualified is he for ministry?

2. What sort of life did Paul have? What drove him to keep going?

3. What is the effect of Paul boasting in his weaknesses?

PONDER What are the things you privately boast in? How do they compare to what Paul boasts in?

PRAYER IDEAS Thank God that his Son has secured heaven for you. Ask him to give you a great longing to follow Jesus as you await heaven.

READING 58   2 CORINTHIANS 12:1-13

I must go on boasting. Though there is nothing to be gained by it, I will go on to visions and revelations of the Lord. 2 I know a man in Christ who fourteen years ago was caught up to the third heaven—whether in the body or out of the body I do not know,

God knows. 3 And I know that this man was caught up into paradise—whether in the body or out of the body I do not know, God knows— 4 and he heard things that cannot be told, which man may not utter. 5 On behalf of this man I will boast, but on my own behalf I will not boast, except of my weaknesses. [6] Though if I should wish to boast, I would not be a fool, for I would be speaking the truth. But I refrain from it, so that no one may think more of me than he sees in me or hears from me. [7] So to keep me from becoming conceited because of the surpassing greatness of the revelations, a thorn was given me in the flesh, a messenger of Satan to harass me, to keep me from becoming conceited. [8] Three times I pleaded with the Lord about this, that it should leave me. [9] But he said to me, "My grace is sufficient for you, for my power is made perfect in weakness." Therefore I will boast all the more gladly of my weaknesses, so that the power of Christ may rest upon me. [10] For the sake of Christ, then, I am content with weaknesses, insults, hardships, persecutions, and calamities. For when I am weak, then I am strong.

[11] I have been a fool! You forced me to it, for I ought to have been commended by you. For I was not at all inferior to these super-apostles, even though I am nothing. [12] The signs of a true apostle were performed among you with utmost patience, with signs and wonders and mighty works. [13] For in what were you less favored than the rest of the churches, except that I myself did not burden you? Forgive me this wrong!

1. Why does Paul say there is "nothing to be gained" by continuing to boast (v. 1)?

2. How was Paul's "thorn" actually helpful to him?

3. Paul says in verse 11 that he has been a fool. What has been 'foolish' about his behaviour? Why has he done this?

PONDER When are you tempted to be impressed by 'experiences'? How do you deal with your own 'thorns'?

PRAYER IDEAS Ask God to give you a clear vision of the power of Christ in all circumstances.

READING 59   2 CORINTHIANS 12:14-13:4

Here for the third time I am ready to come to you. And I will not be a burden, for I seek not what is yours but you. For children are not obligated to save up for their parents, but parents for their children. [15] I will most gladly spend and be spent for your souls. If I love you more, am I to be loved less? [16] But granting that I myself did not burden you, I was crafty, you say, and got the better of you by deceit. [17] Did I take advantage of you through any of those whom I sent to you? [18] I urged Titus to go, and sent the brother with him. Did Titus take advantage of you? Did we not act in the same spirit? Did we not take the same steps?

[19] Have you been thinking all along that we have been defending ourselves to you? It is in the sight of God that we have been speaking in Christ, and all for your upbuilding, beloved. [20] For I fear that perhaps when I come I may find you not as I wish, and that you may find me not as you wish—that perhaps there may be quarreling, jealousy, anger, hostility, slander, gossip, conceit, and disorder. [21] I fear that when I come again my God may humble me before you, and I may have to mourn over many of those who sinned earlier and have not repented of the impurity, sexual immorality, and sensuality that they have practiced.

13:1 This is the third time I am coming to you. Every charge must be established by the evidence of two or three witnesses. ² I warned those who sinned before and all the others, and I warn them now while absent, as I did when present on my second visit, that if I come again I will not spare them— ³ since you seek proof that Christ is speaking in me. He is not weak in dealing with you, but is powerful among you. ⁴ For he was crucified in weakness, but lives by the power of God. For we also are weak in him, but in dealing with you we will live with him by the power of God.

1. What is Paul prepared to do on his third visit to Corinth?

2. How is Christ central to Paul's actions?

3. Does 12:19 cause you to re-evaluate your overall impression of the book so far? Why/why not?

PONDER How prepared are you to "most gladly spend and be spent for [other people's] souls" (12:15)?

PRAYER IDEAS Ask God to change your heart so that your motives for serving other Christians are always Christ-centred.

READING 60   2 CORINTHIANS 13:5-14

Examine yourselves, to see whether you are in the faith. Test yourselves. Or do you not realize this about yourselves, that Jesus Christ is in you?—unless indeed you fail to meet the test! ⁶ I hope you will find out that we have not failed the test. ⁷ But we pray to God that you may not do wrong—not that we may appear to have met the test, but that you may do what is right, though we may seem to have failed. ⁸ For we cannot do anything against the truth, but only for the truth. ⁹ For we are glad when we are weak and you are strong. Your restoration is what we pray for. ¹⁰ For this reason I write these things while I am away from you, that when I come I may not have to be severe in my use of the authority that the Lord has given me for building up and not for tearing down.

¹¹ Finally, brothers, rejoice. Aim for restoration, comfort one another, agree with one another, live in peace; and the God of love and peace will be with you. ¹² Greet one another with a holy kiss. ¹³ All the saints greet you.

¹⁴ The grace of the Lord Jesus Christ and the love of God and the fellowship of the Holy Spirit be with you all.

1. What does Paul urge the Corinthians to do to prepare for his third visit?

2. What do you notice about the way Paul ministers to the Corinthians even though he is not present with them?

3. What (if anything) do verses 11-14 tell you about Paul's agenda for writing?

PONDER Are you of the faith? Is the Christ you know the Christ the apostles proclaimed?

PRAYER IDEAS Ask God to help you open your heart wide to Paul and all that he has written as a result of reading 2 Corinthians.

APPENDIX

ADDITIONAL PASSAGES REFERRED TO ...

Judges 13:2-24 (Reading 2)

There was a certain man of Zorah, of the tribe of the Danites, whose name was Manoah. And his wife was barren and had no children. ³ And the angel of the Lord appeared to the woman and said to her, "Behold, you are barren and have not borne children, but you shall conceive and bear a son. ⁴ Therefore be careful and drink no wine or strong drink, and eat nothing unclean, ⁵ for behold, you shall conceive and bear a son. No razor shall come upon his head, for the child shall be a Nazirite to God from the womb, and he shall begin to save Israel from the hand of the Philistines." ⁶ Then the woman came and told her husband, "A man of God came to me, and his appearance was like the appearance of the angel of God, very awesome. I did not ask him where he was from, and he did not tell me his name, ⁷ but he said to me, 'Behold, you shall conceive and bear a son. So then drink no wine or strong drink, and eat nothing unclean, for the child shall be a Nazirite to God from the womb to the day of his death.'"

⁸ Then Manoah prayed to the Lord and said, "O Lord, please let the man of God whom you sent come again to us and teach us what we are to do with the child who will be born." ⁹ And God listened to the voice of Manoah, and the angel of God came again to the woman as she sat in the field. But Manoah her husband was not with her. ¹⁰ So the woman ran quickly and told her husband, "Behold, the man who came to me the other day has appeared to me." ¹¹ And Manoah arose and went after his wife and came to the man and said to him, "Are you the man who spoke to this woman?" And he said, "I am." ¹² And Manoah said, "Now when your words come true, what is to be the child's manner of life, and what is his mission?" ¹³ And the angel of the Lord said to Manoah, "Of all that I said to the woman let her be careful. ¹⁴ She may not eat of anything that comes from the vine, neither let her drink wine or strong drink, or eat any unclean thing. All that I commanded her let her observe."

¹⁵ Manoah said to the angel of the Lord, "Please let us detain you and prepare a young goat for you." ¹⁶ And the angel of the Lord said to Manoah, "If you detain me, I will not eat of your food. But if you prepare a burnt offering, then offer it to the Lord." (For Manoah did not know that he was the angel of the Lord.) ¹⁷ And Manoah said to the angel of the Lord, "What is your name, so that, when your words come true, we may honor you?" ¹⁸ And the angel of the Lord said to him, "Why do you ask my name, seeing it is wonderful?" ¹⁹ So Manoah took the young goat with the grain offering, and offered it on the rock to the Lord, to the one who works wonders, and Manoah and his wife were watching. ²⁰ And when the flame went up toward heaven from the altar, the angel of the Lord went up in the flame of the altar. Now Manoah and his wife were watching, and they fell on their faces to the ground.

²¹ The angel of the Lord appeared no more to Manoah and to his wife. Then Manoah knew that he was the angel of the Lord. ²² And Manoah said to his wife, "We shall surely die, for we have seen God." ²³ But his wife said

to him, "If the LORD had meant to kill us, he would not have accepted a burnt offering and a grain offering at our hands, or shown us all these things, or now announced to us such things as these." 24 And the woman bore a son and called his name Samson. And the young man grew, and the LORD blessed him.

Isaiah 61 (Readings 13 and 19)

The Spirit of the Lord GOD is upon me,
    because the LORD has anointed me
to bring good news to the poor;
    he has sent me to bind up the
        brokenhearted,
to proclaim liberty to the captives,
    and the opening of the prison to those
        who are bound;
2 to proclaim the year of the LORD's favor,
    and the day of vengeance of our God;
    to comfort all who mourn;
3 to grant to those who mourn in Zion—
    to give them a beautiful headdress
        instead of ashes,
the oil of gladness instead of mourning,
    the garment of praise instead of a faint
        spirit;
that they may be called oaks of
        righteousness,
    the planting of the LORD, that he may be
        glorified.
4 They shall build up the ancient ruins;
    they shall raise up the former
        devastations;
they shall repair the ruined cities,
    the devastations of many generations.

5 Strangers shall stand and tend your flocks;
    foreigners shall be your plowmen and
        vinedressers;
6 but you shall be called the priests of the
        LORD;
    they shall speak of you as the ministers
        of our God;
you shall eat the wealth of the nations,
    and in their glory you shall boast.
7 Instead of your shame there shall be a
double portion;
    instead of dishonor they shall rejoice in
        their lot;
therefore in their land they shall possess a
        double portion;
    they shall have everlasting joy.

8 For I the LORD love justice;
    I hate robbery and wrong;
I will faithfully give them their recompense,
    and I will make an everlasting covenant
        with them.
9 Their offspring shall be known among the
        nations,
    and their descendants in the midst of
        the peoples;
all who see them shall acknowledge them,
    that they are an offspring the LORD has
        blessed.

10 I will greatly rejoice in the LORD;
    my soul shall exult in my God,
for he has clothed me with the garments of
        salvation;
    he has covered me with the robe of
        righteousness,
as a bridegroom decks himself like a priest
        with a beautiful headdress,
    and as a bride adorns herself with her
        jewels.
11 For as the earth brings forth its sprouts,
    and as a garden causes what is sown in
        it to sprout up,
so the Lord GOD will cause righteousness
        and praise
    to sprout up before all the nations.

Psalm 107 (Reading 19)

Oh give thanks to the LORD, for he is good,
    for his steadfast love endures forever!
2 Let the redeemed of the LORD say so,
    whom he has redeemed from trouble
3 and gathered in from the lands,
    from the east and from the west,
    from the north and from the south.

4 Some wandered in desert wastes,
  finding no way to a city to dwell in;
5 hungry and thirsty,
  their soul fainted within them.
6 Then they cried to the Lord in their
    trouble,
  and he delivered them from their
    distress.
7 He led them by a straight way
  till they reached a city to dwell in.
8 Let them thank the Lord for his steadfast
    love,
  for his wondrous works to the children
    of man!
9 For he satisfies the longing soul,
  and the hungry soul he fills with good
    things.

10 Some sat in darkness and in the shadow
    of death,
  prisoners in affliction and in irons,
11 for they had rebelled against the words
    of God,
  and spurned the counsel of the Most
    High.
12 So he bowed their hearts down with hard
    labor;
  they fell down, with none to help.
13 Then they cried to the Lord in their
    trouble,
  and he delivered them from their
    distress.
14 He brought them out of darkness and the
    shadow of death,
  and burst their bonds apart.
15 Let them thank the Lord for his steadfast
    love,
  for his wondrous works to the children
    of man!
16 For he shatters the doors of bronze
  and cuts in two the bars of iron.

17 Some were fools through their sinful
    ways,
  and because of their iniquities suffered
    affliction;

18 they loathed any kind of food,
  and they drew near to the gates of
    death.
19 Then they cried to the Lord in their
    trouble,
  and he delivered them from their
    distress.
20 He sent out his word and healed them,
  and delivered them from their
    destruction.
21 Let them thank the Lord for his steadfast
    love,
  for his wondrous works to the children
    of man!
22 And let them offer sacrifices of
    thanksgiving,
  and tell of his deeds in songs of joy!

23 Some went down to the sea in ships,
  doing business on the great waters;
24 they saw the deeds of the Lord,
  his wondrous works in the deep.
25 For he commanded and raised the stormy
    wind,
  which lifted up the waves of the sea.
26 They mounted up to heaven; they went
    down to the depths;
  their courage melted away in their evil
    plight;
27 they reeled and staggered like drunken
    men
  and were at their wits' end.
28 Then they cried to the Lord in their
    trouble,
  and he delivered them from their
    distress.
29 He made the storm be still,
  and the waves of the sea were hushed.
30 Then they were glad that the waters were
    quiet,
  and he brought them to their desired
    haven.
31 Let them thank the Lord for his steadfast
    love,
  for his wondrous works to the children
    of man!

³² Let them extol him in the congregation
of the people,
and praise him in the assembly of the
elders.

³³ He turns rivers into a desert,
springs of water into thirsty ground,
³⁴ a fruitful land into a salty waste,
because of the evil of its inhabitants.
³⁵ He turns a desert into pools of water,
a parched land into springs of water.
³⁶ And there he lets the hungry dwell,
and they establish a city to live in;
³⁷ they sow fields and plant vineyards
and get a fruitful yield.
³⁸ By his blessing they multiply greatly,
and he does not let their livestock
diminish.

³⁹ When they are diminished and brought
low
through oppression, evil, and sorrow,
⁴⁰ he pours contempt on princes
and makes them wander in trackless
wastes;
⁴¹ but he raises up the needy out of
affliction
and makes their families like flocks.
⁴² The upright see it and are glad,
and all wickedness shuts its mouth.

⁴³ Whoever is wise, let him attend to these
things;
let them consider the steadfast love of
the LORD.

2 Kings 8:7–15 (Reading 22)

Now Elisha came to Damascus. Ben-hadad the king of Syria was sick. And when it was told him, "The man of God has come here," ⁸ the king said to Hazael, "Take a present with you and go to meet the man of God, and inquire of the LORD through him, saying, 'Shall I recover from this sickness?'" ⁹ So Hazael went to meet him, and took a present with him, all kinds of goods of Damascus, forty camel loads. When he came and stood before him, he said, "Your son Ben-hadad king of Syria has sent me to you, saying, 'Shall I recover from this sickness?'" ¹⁰ And Elisha said to him, "Go, say to him, 'You shall certainly recover,' but the LORD has shown me that he shall certainly die." ¹¹ And he fixed his gaze and stared at him, until he was embarrassed. And the man of God wept. ¹² And Hazael said, "Why does my lord weep?" He answered, "Because I know the evil that you will do to the people of Israel. You will set on fire their fortresses, and you will kill their young men with the sword and dash in pieces their little ones and rip open their pregnant women." ¹³ And Hazael said, "What is your servant, who is but a dog, that he should do this great thing?" Elisha answered, "The LORD has shown me that you are to be king over Syria." ¹⁴ Then he departed from Elisha and came to his master, who said to him, "What did Elisha say to you?" And he answered, "He told me that you would certainly recover." ¹⁵ But the next day he took the bed cloth and dipped it in water and spread it over his face, till he died. And Hazael became king in his place.

Numbers 6:1–18 (Reading 26)

And the LORD spoke to Moses, saying, ² "Speak to the people of Israel and say to them, When either a man or a woman makes a special vow, the vow of a Nazirite, to separate himself to the LORD, ³ he shall separate himself from wine and strong drink. He shall drink no vinegar made from wine or strong drink and shall not drink any juice of grapes or eat grapes, fresh or dried. ⁴ All the days of his separation he shall eat nothing that is produced by the grapevine, not even the seeds or the skins.
⁵ "All the days of his vow of separation, no razor shall touch his head. Until the time is completed for which he separates himself to the LORD, he shall be holy. He shall let the locks of hair of his head grow long.

6 "All the days that he separates himself to the Lord he shall not go near a dead body. 7 Not even for his father or for his mother, for brother or sister, if they die, shall he make himself unclean, because his separation to God is on his head. 8 All the days of his separation he is holy to the Lord.

9 "And if any man dies very suddenly beside him and he defiles his consecrated head, then he shall shave his head on the day of his cleansing; on the seventh day he shall shave it. 10 On the eighth day he shall bring two turtledoves or two pigeons to the priest to the entrance of the tent of meeting, 11 and the priest shall offer one for a sin offering and the other for a burnt offering, and make atonement for him, because he sinned by reason of the dead body. And he shall consecrate his head that same day 12 and separate himself to the Lord for the days of his separation and bring a male lamb a year old for a guilt offering. But the previous period shall be void, because his separation was defiled.

13 "And this is the law for the Nazirite, when the time of his separation has been completed: he shall be brought to the entrance of the tent of meeting, 14 and he shall bring his gift to the Lord, one male lamb a year old without blemish for a burnt offering, and one ewe lamb a year old without blemish as a sin offering, and one ram without blemish as a peace offering, 15 and a basket of unleavened bread, loaves of fine flour mixed with oil, and unleavened wafers smeared with oil, and their grain offering and their drink offerings. 16 And the priest shall bring them before the Lord and offer his sin offering and his burnt offering, 17 and he shall offer the ram as a sacrifice of peace offering to the Lord, with the basket of unleavened bread. The priest shall offer also its grain offering and its drink offering. 18 And the Nazirite shall shave his consecrated head at the entrance of the tent of meeting and shall take the hair from his consecrated head and put it on the fire that is under the sacrifice of the peace offering.

Romans 12:9–21 (Reading 33)

Let love be genuine. Abhor what is evil; hold fast to what is good. 10 Love one another with brotherly affection. Outdo one another in showing honor. 11 Do not be slothful in zeal, be fervent in spirit, serve the Lord. 12 Rejoice in hope, be patient in tribulation, be constant in prayer. 13 Contribute to the needs of the saints and seek to show hospitality.

14 Bless those who persecute you; bless and do not curse them. 15 Rejoice with those who rejoice, weep with those who weep. 16 Live in harmony with one another. Do not be haughty, but associate with the lowly. Never be wise in your own sight. 17 Repay no one evil for evil, but give thought to do what is honorable in the sight of all. 18 If possible, so far as it depends on you, live peaceably with all. 19 Beloved, never avenge yourselves, but leave it to the wrath of God, for it is written, "Vengeance is mine, I will repay, says the Lord." 20 To the contrary, "if your enemy is hungry, feed him; if he is thirsty, give him something to drink; for by so doing you will heap burning coals on his head." 21 Do not be overcome by evil, but overcome evil with good.

Acts 15:4–18 (Reading 40)

When they came to Jerusalem, they were welcomed by the church and the apostles and the elders, and they declared all that God had done with them. 5 But some believers who belonged to the party of the Pharisees rose up and said, "It is necessary to circumcise them and to order them to keep the law of Moses."

6 The apostles and the elders were gathered together to consider this matter. 7 And after there had been much debate, Peter stood up and said to them, "Brothers, you know that in the early days God made a choice among

you, that by my mouth the Gentiles should hear the word of the gospel and believe. 8 And God, who knows the heart, bore witness to them, by giving them the Holy Spirit just as he did to us, 9 and he made no distinction between us and them, having cleansed their hearts by faith. 10 Now, therefore, why are you putting God to the test by placing a yoke on the neck of the disciples that neither our fathers nor we have been able to bear? 11 But we believe that we will be saved through the grace of the Lord Jesus, just as they will."

12 And all the assembly fell silent, and they listened to Barnabas and Paul as they related what signs and wonders God had done through them among the Gentiles. 13 After they finished speaking, James replied,

"Brothers, listen to me. 14 Simeon has related how God first visited the Gentiles, to take from them a people for his name. 15 And with this the words of the prophets agree, just as it is written,

16 "'After this I will return,
and I will rebuild the tent of David that
has fallen;
I will rebuild its ruins,
and I will restore it,
17 that the remnant of mankind may
seek the Lord,
and all the Gentiles who are called
by my name,
says the Lord, who makes these
things 18 known from of old.'"